CLEAR CREEK

IN PLACE
Jeremy Jones, Series Editor
Elena Passarello, Series Editor

Curing Season: Artifacts
Kristine Langley Mahler

A Year without Months
Charles Dodd White

American Vaudeville
Geoffrey Hilsabeck

This Way Back
Joanna Eleftheriou

The Painted Forest
Krista Eastman

Far Flung: Improvisations on National Parks, Driving to Russia, Not Marrying a Ranger, the Language of Heartbreak, and Other Natural Disasters
Cassandra Kircher

Lowest White Boy
Greg Bottoms

On Homesickness: A Plea
Jesse Donaldson

CLEAR CREEK

....

Toward a Natural Philosophy

....

ERIK REECE

Photographs by

MORRIS ALLEN GRUBBS

WEST VIRGINIA UNIVERSITY PRESS
MORGANTOWN

Photographs copyright © Morris Allen Grubbs. Used by permission.

"Black Hawk held: In reason," from Lorine Niedecker, *Lorine Niedecker: Collected Works*, edited by Jenny Penberthy (Berkeley: University of California Press). © 2002 Regents of the University of California. Used by permission of the University of California Press.

ISBN 978-1-952271-90-8 (paperback) / 978-1-952271-91-5 (ebook)

Library of Congress Control Number: 2023010655

Book and cover design by Than Saffel / WVU Press
Cover image: *Clear Creek*, 8×10 oil painting © Graham Pohl

for
Jim Maffett,
who taught me the art of curiosity

Leave me this life that paganly passes
on the banks of rivers . . .
—*Fernando Pessoa*

CLEAR CREEK

DURING the summer that I turned forty-five—middle-age by any conceivable standard—I moved to the woods and, with the woman I planned to marry, set up house on a ridge side covered in hickories, buckeyes, and chinquapin oaks—a slope that dropped off over a sheer rock wall, then opened up onto Clear Creek, a beautiful body of water where, along its banks, a small wedding party (bride, groom, preacher, photographer, and witness) could be squeezed onto one large platform of white limestone. The officiant was the pastor of a progressive church started right after the Civil War by the abolitionist minister John Fee. The photographer, Morris, was a friend from graduate school (we had once performed a disastrous scene from *Hamlet* in front of our Shakespeare seminar, a scene in which I, as Polonius, forgot my lines) and the witness was his wife, Anissa, who had baked an apple-caramel pound cake for the occasion. Melissa wore hiking boots beneath her wedding dress—her twin sister's second grievance of the day, the first being that she wasn't invited. After a ten-minute ceremony in which the minister riffed on the theme of our marriage to each other and to this land, we all hiked back up to the house to drink champagne, eat cake, and sign the marriage license. Since Melissa and I weren't members of our officiant's church, or of any church, I slipped him an envelope containing a few large bills. My life had just taken, I could plainly see, a serious turn in the right direction.

IN EARLY SPRING, the five-lobed leaves of the Ohio buckeye emerge from their swollen pink buds like a pair of hands tightly folded in prayer. Then each pair of palmate leaves opens onto another pair, and then another—hands inside hands—waving to us from the western slope below our house, calling us down into this karst terrain. Beneath the buckeyes, twinleaf begins to bloom, a white wildflower with two matching triangular leaves spreading from the tip of its stem. The flowers only last a few days, and then the hillside looks like a swaying congregation of green bow ties. The botanist William Bartram named the genus *Jeffersonia diphylla* after Thomas Jefferson because this spring ephemeral was said to be the third president's favorite wildflower. Jefferson's agrarian romanticism certainly influenced my own move to the rural hamlet of Nonesuch, Kentucky. (In 1901, local journalist Dan Bowmar asked a farmer, Bolivar Bond, how Nonesuch got its name. Bond replied that, because of its reputation for selling whiskey, "it was once called Nonesuch because there was 'no such' place as bad, and now we call it that because there is 'none such' place as good." Today, as then, Nonesuch consists basically of one store—now a gas station and grocery—at a crossroads that leads down to the Kentucky River.) Like Jefferson, I wanted to spend my days thinking and writing, exploring the

countryside and altering it slightly in the name of sustenance. I wanted to abandon the industrial city that was the
legacy of Jefferson's nemesis, Alexander Hamilton. And I
often felt that while most of America was migrating—mentally and physically—toward urban environs, I was heading
in exactly the opposite direction. While most of the country
was running to the city, I was running away from it. I
wanted to abandon Hamilton's economy of commerce for
Jefferson's economy of nature. It *was* a romantic undertak-
ing but not an entirely naive one. I had spent many years as
a very amateur naturalist, exploring and studying the broad-
leaf forests of central and Eastern Kentucky, landscapes and
ecosystems quite similar to Jefferson's own Virginia Pied-
mont. I knew how to tend a vegetable garden, raise and
butcher chickens, cut and split firewood, build a wooden
boat. I taught myself these things in the city, waiting for the
day when I would finally abandon it.

So when the opportunity came, Melissa and I bought this
house on a hillside that is lined at the top with cedars and
hickories and bordered at the bottom by Clear Creek. We
live about a mile off the state route, called Fords Mill Road,
up on a ridge with seven other families, though none can
see another house from its own windows. I say families,
but most are couples whose children are grown and gone.
Almost all of them have been living up here for decades.
There are no fences, and the neighbors have formed their
own unwritten Magna Carta, which says anyone can ramble
on anyone else's land. What this means is that while Melissa
and I lay claim to only five acres, it feels as if we own about
fifty. We can walk all of the trails down by the creek without

fear of trespassing, and our dogs, like all the others up here, can run free.

Our house itself was built about thirty years ago with the most abundant resources on this property: cedar and creek stone. In fact, the builder formed its interior walls with stones that were once part of a dam at the bottom of our land. Records from the Woodford County courthouse say that on June 2, 1789, a certain William Thomas "asked leave" to build a mill on Clear Creek. The remnants of the dam at the bottom of our property impounded water for that mill. A 1901 article from a local newspaper presumes that mill was the first one built in the county. By that point, it was owned by a man named James Ford. The 1901 article describes Ford's home as "one of the handsomest houses in this section of the state." The large gray dwelling, with tall white pillars on an antebellum portico, still stands; we can see it out of our back door when the leaves are off the trees. Ford added a distillery to his mill in the mid-1800s, and there is no place in the world more famous for its bourbon than Woodford County. Melissa had agreed to move to the country with me, but she wasn't, in her words, "going to live in a log cabin." And there are still a lot of log cabins in Kentucky. So when we walked into this house, with its stone walls, exposed pine beams, and beautiful views, Melissa looked at me and said, "This is our house." I looked back and said, "This is our land."

That land is wooded, except for an acre where I have staked out our garden on a bench above the house and built a chicken coop and aviary below it. Along with the dominant cedars, hickories, and buckeyes, I've identified a good number of chinquapin oak, American elm, sugar maple, black walnut, hackberry, cherry, box elder, white ash, hornbeam, and spicebush. An evolutionary biologist might say I have returned to my hominid home, since it was on such a savanna at the edge of an African forest that, about three million years ago, my species stood up to walk on its hind legs, freeing its hands to make tools and build elaborate shelters. And in fact, when I walk through these woods and down beside the creek, I feel two slightly conflicting emotions. One, I can't believe it took me so long to get here. If it had taken Thoreau this long to get to Walden Pond, he wouldn't have made it; he would have already been dead by one year. On the other hand, I feel like my life thus far has been a long trajectory pointing ultimately to this place. I am returning, not to the literal place where I was raised, Louisville, Kentucky, but rather to a more deeply genetic abode. Since I only spent eighteen years in Louisville, and *Homo sapiens* spent around one hundred thousand years wandering the forest edges of Africa, that feels about right to me. I barely recognize my hometown anymore, but something more intrinsic in me recognizes a stand of trees at the edge of a clearing, a creek that flows beneath cutbacks and rock houses.

When people come out to see us, their invariable response, both spoken and unspoken, is: "It's a nice place to visit, but I wouldn't want to live here." I've come to feel exactly the same way about cities. There is much I still like about cities, and I *do* want to visit them: I want to hear their music, check out their art, and drink their fancy cocktails. But it is here on Clear Creek that I finally feel a profound sense of homecoming.

Many years ago, when I made the American nature writer's obligatory pilgrimage to Walden Pond, I bought at the gift shop a bumper sticker that read ALL GOOD THINGS ARE WILD AND FREE, and I affixed it to the back of my truck. One night, while living in Lexington, Kentucky, I dreamed that the staghorn sumacs I had planted in my garden pulled up their roots and followed me out to the country. What I found when Melissa and I finally did arrive here in the country were real stags, white-tailed deer, wandering the fields and woods. Do I feel wild and free now, living here among the deer and raccoons, the coyotes and foxes, the nighthawks and screech owls? What I feel is this: that I have been released into a wild domesticity. "Wilderness," after all, is simply a domestic arrangement we don't understand—the two summer tanagers nesting in our woods, for instance. They are wild and free because they're true to their own nature—domestic and otherwise—as I am now trying to be. The farmer-poet Wendell Berry offers the best definition of wildness that I know: "wild is anything / Beyond the reach of purpose not its own." That, of course, is also a fine definition of freedom. Thus, the tanagers *are* wild and free, as are the skunks and the voles and the hellbenders. But to exist entirely beyond the reach of a purpose that is not one's own—it's something human beings can only aspire to. The summer tanager is born to its nature. We are born divided— divided against our own nature by all manner of cultural, political, and economic constraints.

Yet unlike the tanager, we do not accept our nature as a limitation. We see it as something to be overcome, either through religious faith or faith in our own ingenuity. Thus, we reject both the tanager's definition of wildness and its understanding of freedom. A tanager cannot fly as fast as a hummingbird or use its shorter beak to drink from the deep bell of the trumpet vine. However, the tanager accepts such limitations and lives within its niche. *Homo sapiens* does not. What's more, *Homo sapiens americanus* has developed—more aggressively in this country than anywhere else—a wholly different definition of freedom: one that says coal companies are free to despoil a community's drinking water with toxic mine waste, chemical companies are free to cause birth defects with poisonous herbicides, and anyone in all but six states is free to carry an assault rifle into a grocery store. It's the freedom to not wear a mask during a pandemic, the freedom to refuse vaccination for a virus, though that refusal, along with your unmasked face, might harm and even kill others. In this country, we have somehow misunderstood freedom to mean profligacy, ruthlessness, and irresponsibility. This isn't freedom *from* constraint or suppression—the freedom Thomas Jefferson imagined for the country. It is freedom *to* perpetrate distinct acts of incivility that culminated in the January 6 attack on the Capitol. The best definition of freedom I know comes from John Stuart Mill's *On Liberty*, which states, "The only freedom which deserves the name, is that of pursuing our own good in our own way, so long as we do not attempt to deprive others of theirs, or impede their efforts to obtain it." I believe we can weigh all potential freedoms against this standard—masks, guns, toxic chemicals—and reach a communal, rational conclusion as to whether they impede the freedom of others.

But to speak of freedom in the strictly political sense, I did not come to Clear Creek for the reasons Thoreau went to Walden—to disentangle himself from a corrupt government. I know fully well that my government is corrupt—perhaps irreparably so—but I'm not foolish enough to think it will collapse tomorrow, or to believe I can divorce myself from it. Living in the woods hasn't freed me from the shackles of a government that, as in Thoreau's time, still demands 25 percent of every tax dollar to finance an international war machine. What's more, were I not to pay those taxes, the government would harass me far more than it did Thoreau (who was actually friends with the constable, Sam Staples, who never tried to *re*-arrest him in succeeding years). Though I have physically resisted my government in the past through civil disobedience, and will likely do so in the future, I can make no claims to Thoreau's uncompromising acts of conscience.

Thoreau wrote *Walden* to justify his removal to the woods. I write these pages in part for that same reason, though my circumstances are much different. I have a spouse, a mortgage, a job with benefits. Like Thoreau, I came to the woods looking for something more authentic, and to me more interesting, more beautiful, more satisfying to the senses than what the city has to offer. Like Thoreau, I moved to the country to live more deliberately—that is to say, less distractedly. And like Thoreau, I wanted to wake with nature in an effort to affect my days so they would be worthy of contemplation in the most "elevated and critical hour." But I didn't come here to simplify my life exactly, as Thoreau said he did at Walden Pond. In many ways my life is now more complex—and in ways that I wanted. There are far more domestic chores to do here than in town. There's wood to chop, honeysuckle to eradicate, trails to maintain. I also did not remove myself and Melissa to Nonesuch in an effort to enact the virtues of complete self-reliance. Though I raise a decent portion of what we eat, I am still dependent on supermarkets, an energy company, a fossil fuel industry, and the children of Bangladesh, who certainly made some of my clothes. That is to say, I wasn't driven here by Thoreau's purist principles. I wasn't looking to strip my life to the bare essentials until I was dining on homegrown beans and potatoes. Nor did I come here to act the chanticleer and "wake my neighbors up." Thoreau's smug moral superiority was his least attractive quality as a writer. For myself, I do not think my urban neighbors lead "lives of quiet desperation." Since I'm not a mind reader, nor do I have X-ray vision, I really have no idea what kind of lives they lead in the privacy of their homes and hearts.

But I did come to Clear Creek hoping to free myself from the traffic, the tawdry commercial imagery, the disposable architecture—in a word, the ugliness—of a midsize city that looks more or less like every other midsize city in this country. I did come to Clear Creek looking for the mental and physical satisfactions that I believe can only be found among things that are wild: the wild grapevine, the wild ginger, the wild rushing water. Not that I myself have abandoned popular culture completely; some of it is very good and I think worthy of my attention. But I wanted more frequent and immediate contact with elemental things—things my species didn't create and, so far, hasn't completely destroyed. I hoped that might in turn bring me into more immediate and elemental contact with myself.

A YELLOW WAVE of forsythia has begun to bloom along the top of our western slope. But down below, all along these hillsides that border Clear Creek, the first spring wildflowers are almost all white, the color bees and beetles prefer (butterflies are drawn to the reds and oranges of summer zinnias, bee balm, and Mexican sunflower). Cutleaf toothwort, hepatica, and twinleaf spread in a profusion over the hillside and along the lower trails. The flower of Dutchman's breeches does indeed resemble a pair of tiny white pantaloons. It grows in the lower talus right beneath a limestone cliff where stonecrop and early saxifrage have taken root in narrow crevices. A few bloodroot plants are blooming among the gravel on the creek bank. And one tough little rue anemone has found its way up through a layer of thick cobble. This search for the sun is relentless, even among the smallest flowers. I try to pay careful attention to the quick succession of spring ephemerals as I make my way down our quarter-mile trail to Clear Creek. Thoreau once bragged in his voluminous journal that if he were to fall into Rip Van Winkle's hundred-year sleep, he could, on awakening, tell the date within a week based on what wildflowers were blooming. What Thoreau didn't and couldn't take into account were the effects of climate change on the forest floor. Now, because of warming temperatures, and thanks to Thoreau's exacting records of when each species bloomed in Concord 160 years ago, scientists have found that flowers are blooming, on average, eleven days earlier than in Thoreau's time. Some, during very hot

years, have bloomed up to a month earlier. This could be dire news for both the plants and their pollinators—in Concord and here in Nonesuch—since each would miss out on crucial nutrients and the possibility of reproduction.

Thoreau famously carried on his half-day walks through the woods of Concord a top hat with a built-in compartment to store the specimens he collected. I carry on my back something less inspired but still one of my most important possessions since moving to the country: a folding chair that doubles as a backpack, with shoulder straps and an ample canvas pocket. Most mornings, I fill the pouch with my notebook, binoculars, and a thermos of coffee, strap the chair on my back, then head out. Often, I unfold my little operation on the flat slab of limestone where Melissa and I were married, and I remind myself that the slab is the oldest thing in the state of Kentucky. Or at least a fragment of the oldest thing, Ordovician limestone, which formed during the Paleozoic, when a primordial sea covered what is now called the Inner Bluegrass region of Kentucky. The marine organisms that came to life here extracted from the salt water the calcium carbonite they needed to form their shells and skeletons. Over an unfathomable reach of time, the force of water pressed together the shells of those marine organisms until their remains lithified into limestone. Then, half a billion years ago, a wave of sedimentary rock known as the Cincinnati Arch rose up and rolled from Alabama to Lake Erie. It crested here in the Inner Bluegrass to leave an *anticline*, or dome, formed out of Ordovician limestone. That's why it remains so easy to find brachiopods and tri-lobites embedded in the stone fences that stretch and crumble all across Woodford County. Of the 2,400 square miles of the Inner Bluegrass, Woodford is the only county where almost all of its surfaces and soils derive from the weathering of the limestone.

As for this particular piece of rock where I sit, the roots of a large sycamore have crept out over its surface, and twenty feet away, a long stone ledge extends across the creek to create a shelf of falling water. Behind me, more sycamores and box elders lean out over the pool where the water grows slack and still. Searching for sunlight, their top branches meet the trees from the opposite banks and form a kind of corridor through which the moving water passes. Many mornings, a belted kingfisher makes a quick, reconnoitering loop overhead as he lets loose a vexed rattle, probably directed at me, then disappears upstream. When I moved my office out of doors upon arriving at Clear Creek,

I began writing longhand again for the first time in years. I bought at my university bookstore a stack of the blue books in which I feverishly scribbled answers to final exam questions twenty-five years ago. The blue books are made now, as they were then, by the Roaring Springs Paper Company in Roaring Springs, Pennsylvania. That feels appropriate enough down here, where I can watch at least five lively springs tumbling toward the creek after a good rain. Back in college, the blue books were fifteen cents apiece; now they are thirty. They contain, as the cover informs me, "8 leaves, 16 pages." There's a box at the top of the light blue cover that reads USE YOUR IMAGINATION™. I never noticed it back in school as I awaited and dreaded the exam that was being handed down my row, but now I consider that improbably trademarked injunction as I sit beside the creek. We tend, in this country, to associate the word *imagination* with whimsy, fantasy, escapism. An imaginative child is slightly, if endearingly, untethered from the more mundane realities of his parents' world, and they secretly hope she will grow out of it and eventually go to law school. But for the great American poets Walt Whitman, Emily Dickinson, Wallace Stevens, and William Carlos Williams, the imagination was a vehicle for *seizing* the real, for seeing it more clearly and more intensely. The imagination was a door *through* which we passed back into the experience of our existence; but we passed back changed, more alert and more alive. The true poet captures not just what is seen but the experience of seeing. All poetry, on some level, should be an attempt to transcend the mistake of merely seeing the world as a collection of objects. Poetry should be that place where music, thinking, and seeing meet at an intense intersection of consciousness. Then the poem's borders would dissolve, and the real would tumble into the words that called it into focus. It's as if the mind's eye would become an astrolabe that translates the world into a poem while the words of the poem would become indistinguishable from the things they name. The world and the poem: each would blaze with the light of the other.

THE SYCAMORE IS a water-loving tree that stands on exposed roots all along Clear Creek. On the first day of March, winter wrens flit in and out of the grottos created by that root system, which looks like an enormous octopus rising out of the bank. The tree's dark lower bark turns pinkish as it rises up the trunk before giving way to bone-white branches, which have scattered thin bark plates all across the ground. It's not exactly clear why the sycamore sheds its skin. Some biologists believe the exposed white limbs allow sycamores to photosynthesize light more easily, even when they have no leaves. Where I'm standing, a larger sycamore that leans over the water has sent out its tentacle-like roots to envelop a slightly younger tree three feet away. The latter has reciprocated so that now the two are caught in a vast entanglement. I decide this would be the right place to take in the whole gorge on an early spring afternoon, so I fold myself into a comfortable curve achieved by the two trees' alliance. I lean back against the trunk of the larger tree and prop my feet on the higher roots of the younger one. This arboreal sling is surprisingly hospitable to my human form, and I rest my head against the spongy moss growing up the trunk. Above me, the high white branches sway slightly against a blue sky. Whether they are in a battle or an embrace is hard to say, but their contrast to the firmament is beautiful, and I can feel my breathing begin to slow.

The larger of these sycamores has rotted away at its base so that the thick roots appear like stilts holding up the rest of the tree. One could easily crawl under the tree, between the roots, to wait out a downpour. When I was a kid, I read a book about another boy who ran away from home to live in a hollowed-out hemlock tree in the Catskill Mountains. He was from a large family that lived in a small New York City apartment, so his father wasn't too chagrined to see him go. He had read some how-to-survive-in-the-wilderness books at the New York Public Library, and he appeared quite resourceful and resilient. His door was a piece of deerskin, and his lamp was deer fat poured into a turtle shell. There seems to be something about a child's psyche that loves small, interior spaces: clubhouses, attics, tents made out of blankets. And what could be better than an *interior* tree house? Perhaps for that reason, the book has stuck with me all these years—like a lot of children, I too harbored a notion of running away to live in the woods—and I think of it now, leaning against this hollow tree.

Downstream, right beneath our house, stands what is by far the largest tree in this gorge, a sycamore around which Melissa and I could both reach and still not join hands. The reason it's still here is that sycamores are almost useless to human enterprises. The wood is impossible to split because the tree's xylem cells don't flow parallel as with most hardwoods, but rather swirl to the right one year, then to the left the next. As a result, about the only thing one can derive from a sycamore is a butcher block. Or a nice bower in which to laze away one of the year's first warm days. A kingfisher comes bulleting down the creek until it spots me here and quickly, loudly wheels around. The wrens too seem confused and upset by my presence, which has temporarily displaced their foraging. Across the creek, a moss-covered cutback throws an emerald reflection over the water. I sense the shadow of something over my shoulder, and then a great blue heron appears, slowly winging its way downstream.

Further up the bank, where a wall of limestone levels off, the bare branches of dead cedars contort with Gothic suggestiveness. But for all the living trees, this is the sexual season in the Inner Bluegrass. The hornbeam tree dangles its yellow male catkins right next to the female, who extends her small flowers at the tip of new growth. The red maples are fringed in clusters of scarlet flowers. Down along the bank, silver maples have already sent out their tiny yellow flowers in short-stemmed clusters. The wind will carry pollen to their ovules, and when their fruit sets, the seed will be encased by the largest single wing of all the maples. Those whirling seeds will ride the wind and water in an attempt to get as far as possible from their progenitor. Because sex mixes genes from different organisms, it produces variation, the engine of evolution that creates the diversity a healthy forest needs to fend off parasites.

The great American writer and forester Aldo Leopold famously said that a thing is right when it exemplifies *integrity*, *stability*, and *diversity*, and wrong when it does otherwise.

He could have been talking about a forest community or a human one. The same principles apply. A healthy woodland like this one has integrated its diversity to ensure stability. And while the hardwoods of the Inner Bluegrass are not quite as diverse as the mixed mesophytic forests of Eastern Kentucky—the most varied in North America—I still count far more thriving species than the north woods in either the eastern or western regions of the country. Recent research has found that, through their root systems and fungal networks, trees form a community that communicates with one another and sends nutrients to individually distressed trees. And it makes sense. A tree standing alone falls prey to wind, drought, and insect predators. Trees living together can protect one another, moderate heat and cold, and store a great deal of water. I fix my attention on a boxwood standing nearby. As with these sycamores, moss grows up the base of the tree, then the lichens take over, rising all the way up the trunk. It strikes me now, though it's rather obvious, that a single tree is itself an entire community: mosses, lichens, insects, aphids, flying squirrels, screech owls, wintering birds.

Around four hundred million years ago, plants developed vascular systems to move nutrients around, like the bloodstream in animals. In the competition for sunlight, trees evolved a kind of skeletal heartwood at their core that allows them to rise high above all other plant life. Surrounding that heartwood, vast arteries carry water and nutrients from root to leaf and back. Thus, in two very fundamental ways, we owe our existence to trees. As self-feeding autotrophs, their chlorophyll traps sunlight and splits the H and the O of the water molecule. The O escapes into the air as the oxygen we humans need to survive. What's more, the reason human beings can build houses out of trees is that our ancestors spent eighty million years living in them. When we finally climbed down to stride upright across the grasslands, our hands were free enough and dexterous enough to carry out the wishes of our enlarging brains. We couldn't wrestle or outrun an aurochs, but we could carve spears with our hands. We could even use our hands to paint images on cave walls. We could dominate.

Of course, all that domination has led to a world in which we drill, blast, and scrape 25 percent more resources from the earth than it can replenish. We're living on borrowed time. Our domination has contaminated air, water, and soil, while ratcheting up temperatures to levels that will soon make many parts of the world unlivable. And so in a third way, trees will play a fundamental role if we are to have an inhabitable future. As the earth's greatest photosynthesizers, trees trap carbon dioxide from the air and turn it into nutrients. And a single tree, over the course of its life, can sequester twenty-two tons of carbon. It can also transfer five hundred liters of water a day from the soil, through the leaves' stomata, into the air. Trees prevent 1,200 heat-related deaths each year in American cities. Thus, a tree community also prevents flooding while it purifies air and drinking water. In other words, for no cost, trees are doing a great deal to mitigate the disastrous price of our industrial economy.

Finally, if timber is harvested sustainably, cities could significantly reduce their carbon footprint by building with wood instead of steel. Thanks to the technology known as cross-laminated timber, wooden buildings can now rise to the height of the Statue of Liberty—around eight stories. It takes twelve times as much fossil fuel to create a steel girder as opposed to a wooden beam. And when a tree is converted into timber for building, it continues to store all of the carbon it sequestered during its lifetime. Thus, building with timber would simultaneously reduce the energy that goes into forging steel and reduce the levels of CO_2 in the atmosphere by maintaining carbon sinks in the form of handsome wooden structures. Timber-built housing complexes could slow the clearing of forests for suburbs, while living in such dwellings would provide the unmistakable sense that the woods have come closer to city—that the human community is finally learning something from its arboreal ancestor.

IT'S THE FIRST day over seventy degrees in six months and the first day dry enough to do some real work in the garden, which means tilling under a cover crop of winter wheat, then spreading compost from the chicken coop across my raised beds. Though our land here is largely steep and wooded, there is a flat bench that gets about six hours of sun in the summer. It isn't optimal, but it is enough light to raise a decent crop of tomatoes, beans, cucumbers, peppers, okra, and herbs. When we first moved to Clear Creek, I constructed a vegetable garden up above the house and a chicken coop down below it. Today, a continuous flow of nutrients runs between the three: vegetables flow out of the garden and into our kitchen, kitchen waste flows down to feed to the chickens, chicken manure flows back up to the garden as fertilizer, and garden vegetables flow back to the kitchen as the cycle starts all over again. We of course get eggs from the chickens, and whatever table scraps they can't eat, I compost. It seemed to me a beautiful feedback loop that turned waste into food and food into fertilizer.

So during our first spring here, I built four five-by-twelve raised beds and filled them with topsoil, compost, and worm castings. That was the easy part. Because my neighbor, Jim Maffett, has a tree-mounted, rotary deer feeder that disseminates corn kernels three times a day, we have a lot of well-fed, high-jumping ungulates around here. Unfortunately, they do not seem well-fed enough to stay out of my vegetable garden. The only solution that didn't involve the Pavlovian shock therapy of an electric fence was a seven-foot wood-and-wire enclosure. But the execution of said solution was something of a nightmare. Every time I thrust my posthole digger more than three inches into the ground, I hit solid rock. I tried to break it up with a mattock and only ended up bending the blade irreparably. I attacked the next posthole with a pickax, which sent hundreds of rock shards flying. It was indeed the sound of a man working on his own, self-imposed chain gang. At least that's what my neighbors said as they drove by. But I eventually got twelve posts set and cemented. Then I stretched the fence and framed it in place with one-by-sixes. The word *paradise*, if I'm remembering this right, comes from an Arabic word for "enclosure." In that sense, I finally, doggedly built a modest little *pairidaeza* out of materials bought at my local feed store. I left enough room inside the fence for two Adirondack chairs so Melissa and I could sit and admire my crop with a cup of coffee in the morning and a glass of wine at dusk.

A few weeks after I finished the fencing, my friend Jim Krupa, an evolutionary biologist who has spent his adult life raising all manner of backyard fowl, came out to help construct the chicken coop. The first day, we set cement block footers, framed the basic structure, and enclosed it with plywood. When Melissa got home from work, she said it looked like we'd built an outhouse. But the next day, we attached to it an aviary, essentially a large rectangle made from two-by-fours and wrapped in quarter-inch rat wire. That made the whole lash-up look spacious and respectable; even Melissa acknowledged as much.

Three months earlier, I had placed an order with an Ohio hatchery for fifteen chicks, ten Cornish rock hens and three West Saxon hens. The rock hens would be broilers and the Saxons would live on as layers. I wasn't sure when they were supposed to arrive—the hatchery hadn't said—but one day, I received an agitated call from my local post office. "You've got to get down here right now, Mr. Reece," said the woman on the phone. "These chicks are driving us crazy." When I arrived, she handed me a cardboard container no bigger than a shoebox but perforated and crowded with fifteen thirsty, day-old chicks. The box cheeped all the way home in the passenger seat of my truck. Back in my small shop, I lifted the pullets—ten yellow and three russet—into a three-by-three-foot brooder that I had filled with a bed of pine shavings. The chicks were all smaller than tennis balls, to which they bore a strong resemblance. The brooder was lined with small troughs for water and feed, and it glowed with a red heat lamp. Finally freed from their shipping box, the two-day-old chicks raced around the brooder like little prisoners with a yard pass. I scooped up one after another and held them to my nose, listening to the oddly soothing sounds of their upper-register cheeps. They were impossibly cute and hard to put down. It was harder still to imagine I would be butchering ten of them, the rock hens, in less than three months.

After six weeks in the brooder, I moved the pullets down to the coop. By then, they had enough feather-down insulation to protect them from the lingering cold of March. And they had clearly outgrown the brooder. Each morning for the next month, I slipped the aluminum drop pan out from under their wire flooring and shook an inch-deep layer of steaming guano on the raised beds. I certainly appreciated the fertilizer but was ready to be done with that rank chore. From then on, I would only rake out the hens' droppings from beneath the aviary every month or so, shovel them into a wheelbarrow, and haul them up to the garden or the compost pile.

That's what I'm doing today, pushing about fifty pounds of manure caked in straw up this steep slope. When I groan past the three elm trees in my front yard, I notice the season's first mourning cloak butterfly. Last summer, as a caterpillar, it must have been feeding on the elm leaves. The mourning cloak is one of the few butterflies that actually overwinters here in Kentucky, hiding in a tree cavity or under a piece of bark, so it's also one of the first to appear in early spring, sometimes late winter. Now the insect, in its final, airborne phase, flashes beautiful maroon wings dotted in blue and fringed with gold. Though named for its resemblance to a traditional mourning cloak, the butterfly looks more like a bright harbinger of spring than an emblem of grief. Then again, according to Eastern Kentucky lore, the serviceberry tree (or sarvisberry) got its name because it bloomed in the spring when the ground had finally thawed enough to bury those who had died during the winter. A circuit-riding preacher would come and perform a service, a "sarvis," for the deceased.

All winter long, the foot-high winter wheat had flourished as a thick emerald blanket for the beds, suppressing weeds and aerating the soil. After I empty the wheelbarrow onto the beds, I crank up my tiller, and plow both the brown and green manure asunder. Together, they will add nitrogen, phosphorus, and potassium to the soil. When fighting with the tiller has finally exhausted me, I rake the beds smooth and set out a few rows of radish and spinach seeds. Then I collapse into one of the Adirondack chairs and take it all in. There's something undeniably satisfying about looking over bare, newly planted garden plots. For the moment, they are perfect in their tidiness, their weedlessness, their promise of a good yield. Nothing has gone wrong yet; the garden is perfect in its potential. The soil is well-fed, and life is sleeping there a half-inch below the surface. These dark rectangular beds are like four blank pages, each ready to write into being what Thoreau called the poem of creation.

A GOD WHO speaks through history is very different from a god who speaks through nature. The first god demands collective worship and acquiescence, the second asks only that we listen for the soul in solitude. The god of history demands converts or real estate. The god of nature demands our *attention*.

ON A SATURDAY afternoon, I sit at the base of a thirty-foot white oak and gaze up at this hillside's best secret—a swath of Virginia bluebells blooming right down in the woods on our western slope. My three West Saxon hens scratch and peck through the leaf litter nearby. We are all, in our own way, taking a careful inventory of the forest floor. My gaze is collective as I watch these bluebells spill over a mossy outcrop and then spread down into richer soil. The hens, for their part, examine every square inch before them, hunting most diligently for insects and grubs. Finally, taking their cue, I move in for a closer look. Bumblebees hang clumsily, pendulously from the bluebells, while smaller sweat bees burrow easily into each of the tubular flowers. I find specks of yellow pollen still clinging to the four stamens inside some flowers, while others have given up their male gametes to the bees in hopes of an equitable exchange of food for pollination. Each stem of the bluebells produced a small horn section of pale, papery flowers, perhaps so the heavier bumblebee might brush against one while feeding on another, thus sending pollen grains into the sticky, microscopic clutches of an awaiting stigma. However pollination is achieved, it seems to be working well in this particular patch. Nowhere else on this ridge have I seen such an impressive cascade of March color.

The wildflowers must be beautiful because their sexual season is so fleeting. The flowers must work fast to attract pollinators, and the leaves must breathe in enough carbon dioxide to feed the plant for the rest of the year. Soon, the oaks trees will leaf out and flood this forest floor with shadows. The bluebells, like all of the wildflowers known as spring ephemerals, will only bloom for two weeks, if that, and so I crave their transitory company. Some of my friends and teaching colleagues are spending the day at the Keeneland Racetrack's spring meet, wagering on powerful thoroughbreds, but I like it here among the bluebells. Like those blood horses, they flourish in the Inner Bluegrass because of a soil rich in calcium and phosphorus, the result of its limestone substrate. But unlike the thoroughbreds, these bluebells haven't been tamed or domesticated. They aren't performing for me, though I am taking an ancillary pleasure in their survival strategy: producing beautiful flowers. They are wild, and their beauty is a result of that wildness.

AT DUSK, THE buckeyes' pale clusters of flowers look like yellow lanterns stretched all along the western slope. I walk down the trail beneath them, then into my neighbor's field, where rainwater pools in the abandoned, upturned shell of a box turtle. After strong storms, the creek sounds raucous, suddenly full of purpose. It moves more like an animal, furiously searching out its own disappearance into the Kentucky River a few miles away. Two nights of heavy rain have saturated the ground and called to life even the smallest of seeps. Meanwhile, torrents of water gush from the springs that spread down the cliffsides, then tumble in a white froth over and around the outcrops and scree. More pressurized

hydraulics shoot straight out of the limestone rock walls
that line the creek's outer banks. It's as if a whole under-
world is finally disgorging its secrets. Floodtime is when you
realize how truly porous this limestone country is. One
thinks—or rather one makes the unthinking assumption—
that what lies beneath the topsoil is *terra firma*. But in fact,
the Inner Bluegrass has circling beneath my feet seventy-five
miles of caves, sinking creeks, and subterranean streams.

Clear Creek has risen thirty feet in some places and deposited about a foot of silt below the remnants of Ford's dam
and along parts of the trail. An ironwood tree bends under
the weight of all the dead limbs and debris that collected in
its crown overnight. Four large sycamores have been completely uprooted and toppled. So have several hedge apple
trees, whose bright orange roots stand completely exposed
and look like an angry nest of copperheads or Medusa's ser-
pentine wig. The creek has swept away topsoil to expose the
white roots of wildflowers and flattened for now the toothwort and trillium that was blooming along the banks. What
was a clear, pleasant, and well-behaved stream two days ago
is now a brown leviathan, sweeping indiscriminately toward
an even bigger brown body of roiling water, the Kentucky. In
the narrower stretches of the creek, water pounds the banks,
then rolls back into the mainstream like ocean waves break-
ing backward. One of the creek's tributaries has deposited
what must be at least a ton of white cobble into the creek,
creating a gravel bar almost overnight. I work my way down
to where the single rue anemone was blooming a few days
ago amid loose chunks of limestone. Incredibly, it is still
there, though its pink petals have been pressed flat against

one of the rocks. With my knife, I lift the stem up and brush debris from the flower. When clouds clear away, the chickadees start their racket in the trees along the stream. Higher up, two pileated woodpeckers swoop through the canopy. Higher still, three vultures circle, and above them, a solitary red-tailed hawk rides a thermal that lifts him higher and higher until he is completely out of sight.

Up in my neighbor's field, about twenty feet above normal creek level, I notice a female crayfish that has been badly displaced by the floodwaters. When I pick her up, I find about forty black, fertilized eggs attached to the swimmerets on the underside of her abdomen. The cluster of eggs looks something like a blackberry, which (I discover in a field guide) is why females are said to be "in berry" around this time of year. I walk back to the washed-out creek bank and drop her back down into the rushing water.

I realize now I have been far too sentimental in my thinking about Clear Creek. I have romanticized its beauty without acknowledging its volatility, its destructive nature. But on a day like this, I realize that *water*, far more than anything else, is what shaped this terrain. Clear Creek isn't an afterthought, a tranquil stream meandering along the bottom of these more enduring rock walls. The ruins of Ford's dam are evidence enough that water will only put up with rock for so long. An anticlinal uplift might have thrust all of this limestone into an arch that underlies the rolling farmland of the Inner Bluegrass, but the Kentucky River and all of its tributaries seem determined to find the bottom of that great mass. Clear Creek is the knife that carved this whole gorge in the first place, and it is carving it still.

In the eighteenth and nineteenth century, it was urban malcontents of a literary bent—people like me—who invented the notion of the romantic wilderness, the refuge from squalor, the sanctuary of solitude. Those who actually lived and worked in the countryside—people like the plowman in Bruegel's *Landscape with the Fall of Icarus*—were presumably too busy to gaze up at a distant mountain and think, "How picturesque!" They probably resented the likes of Wordsworth and Coleridge (just as today many sheep farmers resent the movement to "rewild" the Lake District of England; from the farmers' perspective, rewilding for foreign tourists or for abstract notions of conservation just means taking food out of their children's mouths). In this country, it was the ecstatic, mountain-drunk prose of John Muir that first sent urban Americans in search of wilderness redemption. I read those books too, and they sent me on my own extended rambles through our national parks and forests. But by moving to Clear Creek, a landscape that still retains some of its wildness, I wanted to overcome the urban dichotomy that imagines the natural world only as a place to vacation, to recreate, to visit and leave. I wanted to know this landscape intimately, which in many ways is the opposite of romance. When Ralph Waldo Emerson met John Muir on a trip to Yosemite in 1872, the philosopher broke the naturalist's heart by declaring that the solitude of the wilderness "is a sublime mistress, but an intolerable wife." Like Muir, I came to Clear Creek looking not for a fling with nature but for a slowly earned understanding that would last for years and years—hopefully the rest of my life.

A FORMULA: OUR spiritual poverty as Americans exists in direct proportion to our economic wealth and ecological abuse.

I DON'T KNOW if the idea of a morning ritual is particularly American, but I do know Benjamin Franklin put much stock in it. From 5:00 to 7:00 a.m. every day, he would "address Powerful Goodness." My day gets started a little later than that, but I like the notion of beginning with a routine that aspires to Powerful Goodness. For me, it's coffee, binoculars, my notebook, and some classical Stoic text—usually Marcus Aurelius or Seneca—out on the deck. Today, under a cool, overcast sky, I drink my java from the only cup I ever saw my grandfather use. It's a white porcelain mug, hand-painted with strange blue flowers. My grandfather, a Baptist preacher with a deep fundamentalist bent, would sit on his own deck overlooking the Chesapeake Bay and drink one cup of instant coffee after dinner. I came to associate that cup, in some childlike way, with his ministerial authority, with his unquestioned moral rectitude. It became a metonymic extension of a man I loved profoundly. A child of the Depression, my grandfather was a saver who owned very few possessions. My mother always assumed that, since my father, my grandfather's son, had committed suicide when I was three, my grandparents were banking their money to leave to me and my uncle. I suppose she thought of it as a kind of reparation payment to make up for my missing father. But toward the end of his life, my grandfather gave all of his savings to missionaries working to stamp out paganism in South America. This development drove my uncle, already a brittle man, into a vertiginous feeling of betrayal from which he never really recovered. But as someone with pagan tendencies myself—something my grandfather probably suspected—I wouldn't have felt right accepting his patrimony (though I probably would have anyway), and I never gave much thought to the hundreds of thousands of dollars that bypassed me like a Cessna disappearing into the Amazon jungle. After my grandfather's funeral service, I went back to his bayside house—a thirteen-sided structure on stilts that we all called the Round House—and emptied a half-pint of bourbon into his coffee cup. I sipped the warm liquor in bed while I listened to my uncle fume about my grandfather's will out in the main room of the house (which had, after all, been left to him). Then I fell asleep to olfactory dreams triggered by the salty air sweeping in from the bay. The next morning, when I packed, I placed in my bag the one thing I would take to remember my grandfather— that cup. Then I left his home in Tidewater, Virginia, and never went back. Still, I've taken great care of my grandfather's cup with its strange blue flowers, and I drink my own coffee from it every morning.

For some time now, I have thought of myself (and explained myself to others, if they ask) as a Christian agnostic. At some point, I think Christianity got hold of the wrong end of the stick when it chose—as mainstream Christianity always does—to prioritize the book of John over the synoptic Gospels. That is to say, I accept the radical ethical teachings of the synoptic Gospels but not the salvational obsession of John's book, which after all looks nothing like Matthew, Mark, and Luke. I accept and even try to live up to the teachings of a Mediterranean wanderer named Jesus: treat others the way you want to be treated, be humble and magnanimous, forgive debts, stop judging others, return hatred with love, return violence with peaceableness, be merciful. When Jesus said, "Render unto Caesar the things that are Caesar's, and to God the things that are God's," he was saying, among other things, that our spiritual poverty exists in direct proportion to our economic wealth (and, I would add, our ecological abuse). That, I suppose, is why affluent America would choose the easy vision of John 3:16—a free ticket to heaven—over the hard work of following Jesus's actual teachings, as laid out in the synoptic Gospels.

Above the treetops, three crows are mobbing a sharp-shinned hawk. Down here in my Adirondack chair, I hear the cheerful *zzzrrreeeee* of pine siskins. That's followed by the whirring wings of the season's first hummingbird, a male that flashes his sequined red throat for a second at my feeder and then is gone. The hummingbird's arrival signals that the pine siskins will soon be departing, moving north. They've been good winter companions, and I'll be sorry to see them go. On one arm of my chair, a translation of the *Upanishads* sits inadvertently on top of my field guide to Kentucky wildflowers. They are each, I realize, guides to two worlds: one inner, one outer. Each points to the oldest scriptures: one that spreads across the forests and fields of the Inner Bluegrass and one that tried to capture, through pictographic Sanskrit, the soul's own terrain. Swami Vivekananda, the man who introduced Vedanta religion to the United States at the end of the nineteenth century, warned that "books never make religions, but religions make books." Here in the United States, we have indeed vanquished the gods from sacred oak groves and pressed them into books. The problem is that within books, religions often ossify into doctrines and dogma. Religion begins with genius, intuition, imagination, then fossilizes into creeds that get set down in books. The search for God within oneself becomes instead a campaign to impose one's religious views on others. But for Vivekananda, all religions are manifestations of one fundamental religious impulse, what he called "the realizing of God in the soul." To find God within oneself is simultaneously to recognize the one behind the many and in so doing, connect the Vedas to the field guide—the creator (one) to the creation (many). In this view, all of the world's theistic religions are branches of the same tree—different articulations of the original voice that whispers to us of our own divine, though hidden, nature.

My grandfather was indeed convinced of his own superior religion, and he spent his whole adult life trying to impose that vision on others. He once told me that Jews who converted to Christianity in the concentration camps were spared the gas chambers. His dogma, his church, his oppressive certainty eventually made my father's life unbearable, and my father ended it at age thirty-three.* So now, when I read Vivekananda's words, "It is good to be born in a church, but it is bad to die there," I find myself in profound agreement. The ceremonies and symbols of a church are good for children, he wrote, but as we grow, we must become our own individual churches. In the reliquaries of

---

* I've told the whole sad story in my book *An American Gospel*.

the human heart, we light our own candles, burn our own incense, find our own salvation.

In the Baptist church, when you leave one congregation for another, it's called moving your membership. I have decided to move my membership to Clear Creek. I don't mean for that to sound like a complete betrayal of my grandfather, and I don't mean to paint him here as a one-dimensional demagogue. He was a man capable of both great compassion and great cruelty. I once overheard him in his church office giving comfort to his crying secretary, whose husband had left her, and I once heard him denounce his own son, my uncle, in the most profane and revolting terms. He spent hours each week visiting and praying over sick congregants in the hospital, yet he was neglectful and dismissive of my grandmother. The fact is I simultaneously loved and hated him more than any other man I've known. I wanted to please him more than any other person in my life, and when I realized the folly of that, I tried to get as far as possible from his crippling influence. I spent many years trying to be him or trying to be what I thought he wanted, and then I spent many more years trying to be the exact opposite of that. At some point I realized that the second reaction wasn't so much a rejection of my grandfather; it was an attempt to find what my father couldn't—namely, my own way in the world.

Now I hold onto my grandfather through the one possession of his I still have: this coffee cup. But I couldn't hold onto his religious arrogance, his moral certitude, his bitter belief that the wrong son had died. That, I saw, was deadly. When my grandfather died, we were barely speaking. The relationship was badly damaged, irrevocably perhaps, but I was alive. If losing my grandfather's love was the price of learning to live with myself, that was a price I knew I finally had to pay. By walking away from my grandfather's church, I knew I was walking in the right direction, one that eventually led me to the unroofed church of Clear Creek. Here, I decided, I would work out my own metaphysic—a religion that applies only to me.

ON A WARM April night, I can hear spring peepers chorusing down along the creek. It's a high-pitched call that sounds to many like sleigh bells. From this distance, I find it quite soothing, a dependable herald of the season they're named for. So at midnight, I pull on my boots, grab my headlamp and walking stick, then head down toward the creek. I almost don't need the light because above me hovers what some call the pink super moon—a full moon that sits 0.1 percent closer to Earth and thus appears 7 percent larger than usual. But the moon isn't pink. The moniker actually derives from the pink wildflowers, creeping phlox, that now spread throughout our woods. All during the winter, deer kept this trail well worn, making it easy to demarcate even at this hour. When I reach the creek bank, the full moon bathes the limestone bluffs and white sycamore trunks with a pale glow. The crescendo of frog-sound is coming from just up the opposite bank, perhaps near a pond behind my neighbor's stone wall. Spring peepers are part of a subspecies called chorus frogs, who sing by closing their mouth and nostrils, then pumping air from their lungs, across vocal cords and into ballooning vocal sacs. And up close, they really do sound like an amphibian chorus. Different sections of the choir cut in and out with varied modulations of song, like waves of sound that rise and fall. Then some invisible biological conductor calls everybody to a sudden full stop. Silence for several minutes. I think perhaps my own presence might have caused this whole rest (*Man walks among us, be still*). But then the whole *gloria* starts up again.

These are mating calls, of course. During amplexus—the deed itself—a male barebacks a beleaguered female around a still body of water, trying to time his release of sperm with her release of eggs. Once, at a pond in Eastern Kentucky, I picked up a throbbing—truly throbbing—mass of twenty male bullfrogs clinging to one drowning female. And since most frogs are sexually dimorphic, males often end up humping other males to nobody's reproductive satisfaction. But when all goes well, the female will expend around one thousand fertilized eggs into the dark pond. I sit down on the creek bank and listen a long time to the peeping. My eyes have fully adjusted to the night, and now everything— every tree, every vine, every blade of grass—looks like it has been drenched in the silver gelatin compound that some black-and-white photographers use. In the light of the super moon, everything looks slightly eerie, heightened and in- tensified. If one aim of art is to make things appear strange so we can see the real more clearly, then that is the effect of this full moon—acting like a camera's eye through which the sun's refracted light throws this scene into relief. And the spring peepers seem to know it too. They seem to sing louder and longer than usual, serenading the darkness with all the feeling in the world.

To TURN EACH day into a work of art—what would that look like?

ALONG THE TRAIL, the sycamores that were brought low by the flooding a couple weeks ago still struggle to put out one last year of new shoots. Beneath their white tangle of limbs, the wild phlox has now spread like a lavender mist hovering over the valley floor. It softens this scene of twisted trees, displaced cobble, and debris-clogged springs. Red spears of sessile trillium leaves push up through the phlox. A breeze sweeps through the gorge, filling the air with a sudden, redemptive fragrance. Emerald-winged tiger beetles hover a few inches above the ground in front of me, stopping intermittently to copulate (when a priest once asked a famous field biologist what his lifetime of study had taught him about the mind of God, the biologist replied, "He is inordinately fond of beetles"; that fondness, by the way, is something God and Charles Darwin had in common). The trail leads up a natural stone staircase, and at the top of the small cliff, I notice, as I often do, that this one area of staggered limestone shelves and thin soil maintains a far denser and diverse flora than any other place along the creek. The water has cut this limestone at clean right angles as if it were quarried by stone carvers. Perhaps it is the protection of this small, natural amphitheater that has drawn the flowers here into this small refugium. Perhaps diversity begets more diversity. Along with the pervasive phlox and trillium, purple phacelia grows in an inch of humus that the moss has collected onto one boulder. Beneath that, there's Jacob's ladder, early buttercup, golden

Alexandra, false Solomon's seal, wild ginger, rue anemone, ragwort, and fire pinks.

When we walk through an urban garden or an arboretum, we expect to encounter beauty—that's why they were created, after all—but when we come upon an unexpected wild profusion such as this, we don't think of a gardener or of design or of intent. That mysterious unexpectedness is what makes an encounter with this rocky slope of wildflowers feel far more revelatory. Wild bees, tubers, rhizomes, and slow-traveling roots—some a hundred years old—created this microclimate. That is to say: it was *self-created*. To fall back on a common, but to me still potent, trope this is the book of nature that wrote itself, and continues to write itself, into being. It is an original scripture that, though badly redacted by human rapaciousness, can still be partially read and understood by *Homo sapiens*. Much of this language remains indecipherable; we have lost many of the letters, many of the ideograms, and others we have simply never known how to properly translate. Yet still we try, still I try, because in my own theology, there are only two ways to comprehend what we inadequately call the mind of God: we can read the external landscape or we can travel the internal one. In the apocryphal Gospel of Thomas, which many New Testament scholars maintain is older than any of the canonical gospels, Jesus tells his disciples, "The Kingdom of God is inside you and it is outside you." Likewise, I would maintain we can only *know* God in these two ways: through a study of the natural sciences or through our own intuitions that *precede* all language. In other words: science or silence. Priests and preachers have always told us that God proves his existence through inexplicable, paranormal miracles, but the natural world seems to me an everyday revelation, if only we could see it as such. The fallen walnut that I can close my hand around holds within its tough shell an embryonic image of the fifty-foot tree under which I now sit. What other miracle does one need?

Another way to say all of this—another way to find my own credo written in the rocks and the topsoil, the creek and the trees—is that I don't believe God is *a* being but rather Being itself. The Islamic philosopher Ibn Arabi said—and it almost got him killed—that the creation and the creator are indivisible. The Dutch philosopher Baruch Spinoza agreed. So did the Greek and Roman Stoics. They believed that the world is one organism—the body of God, self-organizing and self-regulating. Diogenes Laertius tells us the founder of Stoicism, Zeno, "says that the entire cosmos and the heavens are the substance of god." Spinoza called this entity *Deus sive Natura*—God-or-Nature. Like Ibn Arabi, Spinoza, and the Stoics, I too can only think of God in terms of nature: the Creator-Creation. As for the question at the heart of both physics and philosophy—*How can something come from nothing?*—it means very little if one accepts this view that the creation *is* the creator and vice versa. There was no moment of "creation" because the creator did not ever *not* exist. Indeed, one does not have to speak about "God" at all: to speak about the natural world *is* to speak about God. In this view, the naturalist is no different from the monk. Both are engaged in an ongoing exegesis, both bend to the ground in an endless act of devotion.

I suppose I'm so strongly drawn to this way of thinking

because I want to reject the impulse to look for meaning outside of ourselves, outside of our world. That, it seems to me, was the great error in my grandfather's religion: it denigrated everything in this world—everything beautiful and sensual—so as to make one worthy of the next, ineffable realm. It preached fear and guilt and abnegation. But I want to find meaning, and I want to make meaning, in *this* world. "Whatever else it might be," wrote the Italian genius Roberto Calasso, "the divine is certainly the thing that imposes with maximum intensity the sensation of being alive." William James said almost the exact same thing in his conclusion to *The Varieties of Religious Experience*: "Not God, but life, more life, a larger, richer, more satisfying life, is, in the last analysis, the end of religion. The love of life, at any and every level of development, is the religious impulse." To me, that is the definition of a religious practice: to experience the world with the same depth and intensity we feel before the greatest works of art. To say something is holy is really only to say that it gives life meaning, that it gives living an intensity. Only *Homo sapiens*, as far as we know, makes meaning. And the only reason, it seems to me, to be a meaning-making animal is to use that meaning as a method to better inhabit the world, to better inhabit one's skin. The next world can take care of itself, especially since if nothing can exist outside of the creator, then the next world *is* this world in another manifestation, another embodiment.

The Stoics extended their physiological argument to say that if the laws of nature are the laws of God, then our greatest chance of finding contentment is to adjust our own inner laws to those of nature. "*Zen kata physin*" was their creed:

live according to nature. Years later, Spinoza offered a brilliantly concise paraphrase of this idea: "The greatest good is the union that the mind has with the whole of nature." To know the nature of the outer world is simultaneously to know the nature of the inner world, said the Stoics and Spinoza. Each is a reflection of the other, as if our solar plexus were a two-way mirror. Since the natural world follows the active principle that is God (we could also call it evolution), and because we are part of nature, there can exist no conflict between living according to our own nature and living according to the whole of nature. The Stoics invented the word *cosmopolitan* to mean not an urban sophisticate but rather a citizen of the entire cosmos, a citizen of the natural world. To live according to one's own nature is the microcosmic version of life according to nature, the macrocosm. However, unlike the Stoics, I don't interpret this to mean that nature is inherently "reasonable" or "good" and that we can learn goodness from watching, say, wrens building a nest together or leaf-shredders turning forest duff into topsoil. The natural world is fundamentally amoral. Rather, I interpret *zen kata physin* to mean that first, we must reject the world-negating theologies at the heart of so much monotheism. Then we must realize that our species has coevolved with the natural world—we climbed down from trees to wander the African savanna, to hunt on the veldt, then to sit around fires and tell stories of the hunt—and therefore, our own happiness can best be cultivated by accepting and embracing that symbiosis. It's not a question of what's right or wrong; it's not a question of whether nature is good or evil, fallen or redeemed. It is first and last a question of *adaptation*. The better we understand and work *with* our surroundings, the greater our chances of one, survival, and two, contentment. We are most content when we *adapt*, when we allow our inner nature to reflect the laws of the biological world where we spent most of our genetic history as hunters and gatherers. The great problem with traditional Christianity is that it refuses to let us be what we are; it wants us to be angels and so won't allow us to be the talking, thinking, storytelling animals that we evolved to be. Christianity wants us to reject both the natural world and our own human nature. It always fights our human instincts, never acknowledging that those instincts might have a crucial evolutionary purpose. And a crucial role in our own well-being. I am talking about the version of Christianity handed down by the Apostle Paul, not the one preached by a Mediterranean wanderer named Yeshua, who had a sublime understanding of what it meant to *live* moment to moment in the soul's divine light. The message of Yeshua, Spinoza, Ibn Arabi, the Stoics—and for that matter the wildflowers of Clear Creek—is this: We don't need to postpone the kingdom of God; we simply need to *recognize* it all around us. Religion is useful insofar as it calls us back into *this* realm—that it finds the holy right here. The great mistake of modern Christianity is the belief that the divine is *somewhere else*.

I have been speaking of the psychological and the physiological realms here, but if we accept the idea that the creation *is* the body of the creator, then an entire ethics follows as well (poet Nathanial Mackey has spoken of an "Earthical church"). While the natural world is amoral, there still remains an ethical imperative to live nondestructively in its

presence. We should understand the extinction of species—
one-third of which we could lose in the next fifty years—
as equivalent to making irreplaceable redactions of holy
scripture. Like the Stoics, we should interpret "live according to nature" to mean expanding concerns for our own
self-preservation to include the preservation of the greater
whole—the natural world of which we are, or should be,
an integrated, not an isolated, part. Instead, Christianity's
moral rejection of that world as fallen, as separate from
God, has led to our subsequent and calamitous abuse of the
natural world. Nowhere is this more obvious and odious
than in my home state, where churchgoing coal operators
have poisoned the air and the water of Eastern Kentucky to
such an extent that birth defects of children born near strip
mines are 38 percent higher than those of children born in
other rural areas. But to understand the creation as indistinguishable from the creator would make such land abuse
an ignoble sacrilege. And the healing of that land would
become a religious calling.

To BECOME MORE fully human would mean to become
more fully *animal*, perhaps even more fully rock, stream,
tree, humus. Human—humus. Soil—soul.

I WAKE AT first light, pull on a jacket, and head out for a
walk down our lane, then along Sellers Mill Road. It's a very
narrow two-lane that cuts across remnants of the rolling
woodland pastures that spread all across the Inner Bluegrass once you get away from the steep slopes of creeks and
rivers. The cool air snaps me into a heightened state of

alertness, and I pull on a thin pair of gloves. There is little traffic along the road at this hour. The few cars that have driven through crushed fallen mulberries into a purple past. The more muted violet flower called Miami mist is blooming effusively in the rocky culverts and on the steeper roadside. Soon, I'm passing through a colonnade of trees that line each side of Sellers Mill: chinquapin, hackberry, ash, black locust. The bark of the mature locust is quite distinctive, like thick pieces of loosely braided rope. All together, these trees have created an active avian corridor. Rarely do I see a greater variety of songbirds than on this particular stretch of road. Today, a solitary gnatcatcher is darting from one side of the road to the other. Meadowlarks and red-winged blackbirds are diving down from power lines. Goldfinches flit in and out of the sadly invasive honeysuckle. Two bluebirds dive for insects from a fence rail. A pair of orioles are trying to keep a low profile among the chinquapin leaves, but that's impossible given their pulsing orange plumage. A few hundred feet later, I spot their nest dangling from a high limb like a woven gourd. The female oriole weaves the nest out of intertwined grasses and other fibers with her beak. The round pouch at the bottom has a narrow opening and is often lined with soft matting from milkweed pods.

The wind moves through the tall grass of one pasture, where sleeping cows look like rounded black boulders. Up on a rise stands a shambling old barn with a badly rusting roof and grain silo. Great green swells of tall grass sweep gently away from it like a pulsing vernal sea. In a month or so, the blue hues of wild chicory will replace this muted green. Three ancient bur oaks stand unmoved among all of that movement. Across the road, a bosque of oaks and hickories marks the place where a carefully tended farm gives way to a tree line that delineates a small tributary of Clear Creek. I watch a blue heron sail above the trees, following the contours of the stream.

These woodland pastures are the most characteristic feature of the Inner Bluegrass. This mixture of open grassland and mature trees amazed the first white settlers. When Daniel Boone and his band of long hunters first came through this part of Kentucky around 1770, he called it a "second paradise." And he wasn't alone in that thinking. Sixty years later, James Hall wrote in *Western Monthly Magazine*, "The surface is not broken by hills, nor is it level—but of the beautifully rolling or undulating character, which is, above all others, the most pleasing to the eye."

How did mature trees *and* a savanna-like grassland manage to come together in such a rare commingling? One clue lies a few miles from here in a grotto called Welsh Cave. In 1965, archeologists discovered there an incredible array of mammalian species dating back possibly thirteen thousand years. They found dire wolves, flat-headed peccary, a mammoth—all now extinct. They found other species that now only live on prairies or savannas: the badger, the pocket gopher, the thirteen-lined ground squirrel. One conclusion researchers drew from Welsh Cave is that thirteen thousand years ago, the Inner Bluegrass was a boreal semiprairie. But when the prairie-loving mammals moved on or went extinct, there still remained the great bison herds. When frontiersman Simon Kenton came through as a teenager in 1771, the buffalo traces were so large he had to climb trees to avoid being trampled. From one prospect he counted 1,500 of these docile, woolly maned ungulates looking for cane, grass, springs, rivers, and natural mineral licks. They would graze one place—a "stomping ground"—reducing cane and grass to stubble, then migrate further on, not returning for years. Once the bison were gone, tree seedlings would germinate the next spring. With little competition from the grasses and the cane, the seedlings grew rapidly. Then, when the bison returned to graze again, the trees were mature enough to withstand the stomping. The result was a rare open woodland, something resembling what I'm walking past this morning. And meanwhile, the thundering herds had created buffalo trails that served as early roads and eventually became the routes of state and federal highways connecting Louisville, Lexington, Frankfort, and Northern Kentucky.

The Indigenous people who hunted the bison mostly left the region by 1754, following a twenty-year drought, something common in karst terrain because of limestone's solubility. When European settlers followed the trail Boone had blazed through the Cumberland Gap, Boone himself became incensed at how wantonly they slaughtered the buffalo (packing no salt, they could save little of the meat). He assembled delegates from the four Kentucky settlements at Fort Boonesborough in 1775 to pass a resolution preserving the bison as well as the elk that obligingly followed their paths. But ten years later, a certain settler reported that all the buffalo were gone from this county where I'm walking—Woodford. What took their place, of course, were fenced cattle and sheep that quickly overgrazed the native canes and grasses. But presumably, the settlers wanted the mature

pasture trees to shade their livestock and add an element
of the picturesque to their landholdings. What's more, they
started to furiously plant hemp, a crop that doesn't exhaust
the soil like corn or tobacco, and which helped maintain
much of the character of the woodland prairie. By 1849,
over half of the nation's hemp came from the county where
I now live and the ones surrounding it. Remarkably, 170
years later, after the 2018 federal Farm Bill removed hemp
from a list of controlled substances, Kentucky farmers are
growing it again, making four times what they can on corn
and soybeans.

I stop and take a good look at a lone bur oak. It's been
recently struck by lightning and seems to finally be suc-
cumbing to the battering winds from which it finds no protection. As the great Kentucky naturalists Mary Warton and
Roger Barbour have pointed out, whenever one sees a bur
oak growing alone in what looks like a savanna grassland,
one is looking into the deep ecological past. One is looking at something nonhuman or, rather, prehuman. If I block
out the road and the barn, I am looking at a scene that
resembles this land when it belonged only to the quadru-
peds. They made it what it was; they made it what this is—a
woodland savanna, something seldom seen throughout the
entire world.

To BELIEVE IN nothing is to believe in the earth's intelligence.

To MY LEFT, as I drive to my teaching job at the University
of Kentucky, a full moon rides high in the early morning sky

while thin pools of fog settle down inside the shallow pockets of these bluegrass pastures. To my right, the red sun hovers at the horizon over my other shoulder while I split the difference, driving this narrow two-lane past farms and fields. Often, when I pass by my neighbors' creosote-black wooden fences, I think of the Kentucky-born slave William Wells Brown. This country's first Black novelist, Brown learned to write his name by spelling it with a piece of chalk over and over as he walked along the black planks of some Lexington horse farm in the early 1840s. I like to think that just by signing his name here, he was actually, like a landscape painter, creating the terrain that rose all around him. And what did he do when he was finished with these vast compositions? He ran. He escaped into them and was gone.

SHORTLY AFTER MOVING to Clear Creek, I began to notice a figure moving through my mental landscape that I have come to call the Reclusive Socialist. He's a lot like me. Except he's read more Marx and Gramsci, turgid tomes I could never get through. He has thought more deliberately and rigorously about exactly what he believes. I admire that in him. He always stops after his second drink. I admire that too. He doesn't let books pile up half-read on the nightstand. He takes careful notes on what he reads and won't talk about things he doesn't know anything about. I imagine him as single and living alone in a tenant house somewhere up the road. I think he lives within his means. I heard he once held an academic job but quit over an ethical issue involving corporate patenting of university research. On my walks, I've seen him talking to horses over the fence. We

never speak. Instead, I find his poems rolled up and carefully
wedged in the snag of an old tree or under a stone outcrop.
I've begun collecting them because I'm afraid he doesn't. He
seems to be simply writing on water. Here's one of his poems
I found today:

> The great stone wave
> crested in this karst country,
>
> where I ride it still,
>
> clinging to trees
> like the masts of ships
>
> as the wave sweeps me on
> through a time so deep
>
> chronology collapses
> and I tumble into
> this endless present,
>
> where Han Shan
> is writing his poem
> on a limestone wall
> with a piece of burnt pine.
>
> I stand in a room
> made of rain
>   and read:

"This life is only a spark
knocked from gneiss."

And I feel that too

just as the rain
begins to erase
the poem

that was really
the only thing
holding me here.

———

OUT WALKING THIS morning, I find standing on the creek bank a miniature house made out of creek stones. A small turret rises up from the middle, surrounded by a ring of rocks set on their sides to form a kind of garrison. This, I've come to learn, is the work of my neighbor, Paul David Atkinson, a photographer who likes to stack flat rocks and then take pictures of his creations. In doing so, he enacts two art forms: one of the most primitive (stacking stones) and one of the most contemporary (photography). Of course, he's hardly unique in this. Anywhere you find humans and rocks, from the bottom of the Grand Canyon to the top of Maine's Mount Katahdin, you see such altars of weather-hewn stone. On a basic level, such stacking simply says: *I, a human being, was here, and this is a small monument to my presence.* But surely there's much more than that at work, at play. This stacking seems to satisfy something so elemental in our human psychology that it almost exists beyond the reach of archeologists, anthropologists, and psychologists. But whatever else it means, it represents the beginning of art. Campfire flames probably taught us to dance, and birds probably taught us to sing, but this superfluous stacking must mark the beginning of what we now call the plastic arts.

The origins of narrative art lie elsewhere. On that score, the argument I find most compelling comes from John Casey's novel *The Half-Life of Happiness*, where one of the characters, an anthropologist named Edmond, tells the story of a young male orangutan he once observed in the wild. As soon as the young ape made his first male hooting sound, his mother drove him out of her own territory, as is orangutan custom. But the one-year-old ape appeared distraught and confused as he stumbled from one glade to another. But then he stopped and began to reenact the traumatic scene— playing both roles—that just happened between mother and son. "What I like about my little orangutan," explains Edmond, "is he did something extraordinary. And he did it consciously. He had the worst day of his life, and he didn't collapse—he invented drama." And *that*, it seems to me, might be the real birth of tragedy.

But the act of *making* art, of manipulating materials— that impulse must have begun with these temporary stone totems. Perhaps we do more rock stacking in remote places because there we feel most alive, most exhilarated, most connected to our more primal selves. If so, then Paul David is trying to bring that exotic experience back to the quotidian level of the everyday. Something similar, though much grander in scope, happened in Hauterives, France, in the nineteenth century, where a postman named Ferdinand Cheval walked twenty miles a day delivering letters. There appears to have been nothing extraordinary about him. Then one night he dreamed of a palace, a "chateau of grottoes" so beautiful that he carried the image of it throughout his waking days for fifteen years. Then, in 1879, while walking his rounds, Cheval tripped over a rock and fell, scattering the mail. When he gathered up his letters, Cheval also picked up the offending rock. It was a piece of limestone "shaped by water and hardened by the power of time," Cheval wrote many years later. Because Hauterives sits in an alluvial valley, the result was a "sculpture so strange that it is impossible for man to imitate." But, Cheval decided, "since Nature is willing to do the sculpture, I will do the masonry and the architecture." He put the rock in his pocket and took it home. And that piece of limestone was the first element of what would eventually become an incomparable manifestation of Cheval's phantasmagorical dream. For the next thirty-three years, the postman picked up stones that suggested to him some evocative form. When his wife complained about constantly repairing his pockets, he began carrying a basket. Eventually, he started pushing a wheelbarrow on his rounds, collecting stones and shells as he went. Slowly, what he called his Palais Ideal rose from the ground in his backyard, though the postman apparently had no training in architecture. Perhaps because of that, the Ideal Palace has no discernible influences. It rather falls into the inadequate categories of "naive art," "outsider art," "visionary art." More than anything, it looks like a rococo sandcastle extrapolated onto a monumental scale. Three "giants," as Cheval called them, guard the palace into which they have half-melded. Wearing a kind of chain mail made from small flat pebbles, this triumvirate looks like long shadows cast into stone and mortar. They are neither gods nor angels nor saints. They are rather the guardians of a private vision, a hallucination purified by the builder's persistence, his allegiance to a dream that had to be grounded in stone, a castle that had to be wrestled from the air.

It all calls me back to the question that Paul David's cairns are asking on a much more modest level: *Why?* Why must humans stack rocks, build grottoes, make art? These cairns are clearly totems, but totems to what? Not to any gods, I don't think, either pagan or otherworldly. Nor do they seem to have any shamanistic, psychotropic origins, as many anthropologists now believe inspired the earliest cave art. The postman Cheval and the photographer Paul David seem to have been acting out of a similar impulse. There is no *reason* to do it. The stacking is also anonymous—no one signs a cairn—and therefore it is devoid of self and the infamous artistic trappings of ego. The cairn is impermanent; we know rushing waters will soon level it. And yet we sense, somehow, that this stacking must be done. Like stars in a constellation, one rock must be placed in relation to another. A gravitational tension must hold them together, but also an aesthetic tension. This is the origin of composition, of finding a way to make disparate elements cohere within some kind of structure, some kind of logic—even if that logic is an intuition understood only by the builder, the maker, the artificer.

Are we taking the elements of the creation (a noun) and reenacting that original act of creation (a verb) on a human scale? Are we playing god, answering the macrocosm with our own microcosm? Are we taking stone fragments of what once was whole, in this case bedrock, and recreating our own version, our own understanding of order, of symmetry? As with the postman Cheval, the original art instinct must have begun with a sense of wonder about what one found at hand, at foot. That original art instinct must have been simply celebratory. It is an impulse to engage the world on a basic, nonutilitarian level. It's a way of saying we are ultimately of the same original substance, the warm, sensitive body and the hard, unfeeling rock. We both belong here, belong together. The stacking is a sign of that symbiosis.

When I ask Paul David why he stacks rocks, he shrugs and simply says, "It's therapeutic." But why is it therapeutic? Perhaps because there is an element of sheer *play* involved that is often absent from adult life. Certainly in the world of moneymaking and promotion seeking, Paul David's rock stacking is almost ridiculous, childlike. But therein must lie some of its restorative nature. What's more, the simple experience of placing one stone on top of another seals one inside the present. That moment of making is what matters. Beyond that, the sheer physicality of the act might be part of its tonic. In stacking, Paul David is calling mind and body, thinking and doing, into accord. By extension, the complex structure of the human hand was key to defining us as a species. As archeologist Nigel Spivey has noted, the big toe of our forebearers, the australopithecines, allowed them to rise up with balance and walk on two legs four

million years ago. That, as a consequence, freed up the hand
to form triple-phalanged fingers and wide-set thumbs. What
did we do with these hands? We made art. Like the orangutan, perhaps we mammals with larger brains need the aesthetic form of art to make sense of what seems senseless—a
mother casting away a son, a physical world that appears
chaotic, a scattering of stones.

It's been twelve weeks since I brought home the two-day-
old pullets. Now, like adolescents, they are no longer so
adorable. They strut around on reptilian feet and start to
make a racket at 5:00 a.m. Plus, I can't really afford to keep
the rock hens much longer. They are going through fifty-
pound feed bags like nobody's business. As a result, their
breasts have grown so large they can barely walk. Of course,
they were bred this way, bred to be broilers.

Still, the butchering isn't easy, so I call up my biologist
friend Jim Krupa, who helped me build the coop six weeks
ago and is solely responsible for convincing me I needed
backyard fowl in my life. "At that weight, they'll have heart
attacks and die if you don't kill them," Jim says cheerfully
over the phone. "It's the right thing to do."

In the name of science and scientific specimens—and in
the name of eating—Jim has probably killed at least one of
just about every vertebrate in North America. We share a
similar food politics. Because we can't quite bring ourselves
to become vegetarians, we believe that we should look our
food in the face—at least some of our food—before we eat
it. And when you hold a shrieking ten-pound chicken over
a chopping block, with the hatchet raised in the air, you do

have one doleful moment to look that animal in the eye and take full measure of the task at hand. The sacrifice could not be made more clear.

One by one, I pull the rock hens from the coop and hold their bodies still while Jim administers the death blow that severs the head. A thin stream of blood issues from the neck and turns the grass crimson. The headless torsos convulse for about a minute in my hands. Then I lay each one in a row on the ground, and Jim pairs each head with its lifeless body. He weighs each chicken with his grandfather's copper hand scale that dates back to the Civil War. Unbelievably, the thing still works. Jim records the numbers in a small field book: eighty pounds overall. He then puts each head in an individual ziplock bag and gives it a letter, *A* through *I*. Next week, he will place the heads in a terrarium of flesh-eating beetles, and when those voracious insects have done their work, Jim will hang all of the skulls together in what will look like a pretty terrifying Christmas ornament. There's science behind this, he tells me, measuring variation within and between species of galliform birds. He'll use the skulls as part of a demonstration in his vertebrate zoology class next semester at the local university where we both teach. The truth is Jim likes to turn everything into a science project. In the age of computer simulations run in the name of science, he's an old-school naturalist who loves fieldwork and who harbors acute disdain for lab-driven molecular biology. His heroes are Charles Darwin, E. O. Wilson, and Teddy Roosevelt. He's one of the most popular professors at the University of Kentucky, though it pains him considerably when students tell him he bears a striking resemblance to

George W. Bush. Last year, Jim wrote "Defending Darwin," a spirited essay about teaching evolution at a red state university. It went viral. The online responses were brutal, which delighted Jim. You want to debate evolution versus creationism? Jim will meet you anywhere, anytime.

We carry the carcasses up to the house and take our seats on two upturned plastic buckets. Melissa virtually sprints to her car and clears out, having decided this is an excellent morning for visiting her mother's assisted living facility. And it's true: few things stink quite like the entrails of a chicken, especially on a hot day. First, we cut off the legs and wings at their joints, then peel off the skin and feathers. Melissa has made known her preference that we leave the skin on in the name of keeping the meat moist while cooking, but Jim has also made it known (quite rightly) that plucking chickens is a colossal pain, and we aren't going to do it unless Melissa offers to help. So the chickens are getting skinned.

We make a short incision above the cloaca, then pry out all the internal organs. Jim will take the hearts and gizzards home for dinner; I swore off organ meat when I moved out of my parents' house long ago. But Jim will eat almost anything. He could write a cookbook on preparing roadkill; snakes alone would be one chapter. The only animal meat Jim says he couldn't choke down belonged to a barred owl.

Once the hens are gutted, we clean their carcasses in the kitchen sink, then wrap them in cellophane. I can't convince Jim to take more than one home as payment. So I stack the rest in our deep freezer, beside the butchered lamb I just bought from a local farmer. Melissa and I will eat well in the upcoming year.

I realize, of course, that everything in this freezer was once alive and now is not. I took no pleasure in killing the hens; indeed, I had been dreading it for weeks. But I also know that these animals led decent lives, often free-ranging. They were not mistreated, and they died quickly. Once, at a dinner party, a colleague accused me of something like barbarism when I told him about my chicken enterprise—this while he held a plate stacked with chicken salad on crackers. That to me is a dangerous level of denial, made possible simply by distance. This man thought that his distance from the death of the chicken he was eating absolved him of responsibility, but it only reinforced his complicity in an industrial system of slaughter he was willfully trying to ignore. So at least I have avoided that level of hypocrisy.

But can I mount a better defense of my carnivorous ways? Well, for one thing, if we never butchered chickens, the world would be overrun with them; there would be no place to stand. It is simply unsustainable to have a world where domestic animals are never killed. What's more, very little fossil fuel use went into raising the chickens and grass-fed lamb, far less than goes into much highly processed vegetarian cuisine, and certainly less than beef cattle raised on industrial corn in feedlots. The manure the rock hens produced—and it was substantial—will eventually end up as an amendment to the soil in my vegetable garden, which will allow me to raise organic vegetables to supplement my diet of fowl. And what Melissa and I don't eat from the garden will be fed back to the chickens.

Of course, none of that may be at all convincing to a vegetarian. Carnivores like me can quickly twist ourselves into knots trying to justify the taking of an animal's life, searching for an ethical imperative to meat eating. And too often it can all sound like a petulant defense of the status quo. I understand that. But still, there are right and wrong ways to eat meat. For me, eating animals that have been injected with antibiotics or growth hormones is wrong; eating animals that have been cruelly treated in feedlots and other confined areas is wrong; eating animals whose confinement creates unsanitary and unsafe manure lagoons for surrounding communities is wrong; eating animals that were rendered under unsafe conditions for workers or sold to me by workers who don't make a living wage is wrong; eating animals that are force-fed something—corn and soy—their stomachs didn't evolve to digest is wrong; eating animals that subsist on an ecologically unsustainable crop—corn again—is wrong; eating animals that further contribute to climate change through an intensive use of fossil fuels—fertilizers, pesticides, transport—is wrong; eating animals that contribute to desertification, deforestation, or the destruction of Indigenous cultures is wrong. This is just my list, the one with which I try to hold myself accountable. But when you look at such a litany of *Thou shalt nots*, a list far from comprehensive, you realize how truly difficult it is to eat meat ethically, even with the question of taking a life completely off the chopping block.

Yet really, the question isn't only about killing other living things that possess a nervous system; it's about destroying the ecological structures that support all life on this planet. That's what our industrial food system does: it breaks down and washes away topsoil, it clear-cuts forests, it pollutes drinking water, and because it is driven from first to last by oil and oil-based inputs, it causes climate change faster than anything besides transportation. The way to step outside such a chain of abuse is to either raise one's own food or to buy it from a local farmer or farmers market.

But beyond all of these ecological concerns, perhaps the bottom line for me is this: By raising my own food, or by eating food raised locally by someone I know, I better appreciate what I am eating. I would like to think I understand how difficult it is—physically, ethically, psychologically—to made a chicken breast appear on my plate. Still, when I share a meal with a vegetarian, an immediate divide opens between us: *you eat murdered animals and I don't.* And though of course I don't say it, I want to respond, *yes, I am willing to kill an animal because death is part of life.* I don't mean that glibly. I simply mean it is a fact that we are all going to die. The only difference is I don't know when I will, but I do know when my hens will. But what matters is that we both lived a good life, and I believe these chickens did. They enjoyed fresh straw, a spacious aviary, and woods in which to forage. A Cornish rock hen dies at three months because she has been bred to die at that time. A laying hen will die when she is finished laying, which might not be for six years. By then, her meat will be tough, but I will boil it for hours into a soup; I won't waste it. I will honor her life in the thanks I give for her death.

IF MARCH IS the month of wildflowers, April is the month of wild birds in Kentucky, and it seems as if the migratory warblers all arrived overnight. After a winter of hearing mainly the wrens' and cardinals' constant chatter, now the treetops are full of song. Down in the woods, a pair of summer tanagers have returned to claim the same spot where they raised their brood last year. The male periodically hurls himself into his own reflection in our bedroom window. He's defending his territory and his mate against a perceived rival, though (as is so often the case with us humans as well) the perceived enemy is actually the self. The scene reminds me of a poem about this very subject by the great Kentucky letterpress printer, Gray Zeitz. As a male cardinal bangs and bangs against the window of Zeitz's print shop, the female calls from her cover in the hedge: "You fool. You fool. / I'm true! I'm true!" And in the case of these tanagers, she is. This same pair has returned to this same copse of trees every year we've lived in Nonesuch.

A pair of great crested flycatchers are diligently building a nest in the wooden box my neighbor, Jim Maffett, built for them. At one point, they tangle with a pair of orioles, but the latter soon cede territory to the flycatchers. Higher up, a solitary oriole works his way along the end of a buckeye branch so he can tenuously pluck at its long cluster of flowers. Two male rose-breasted grosbeaks chase each other through the locust trees where my feeders hang. Because of their scarlet breasts, the grosbeaks have been unfortunately impaled on the human myth of bleeding hearts. One legend even says that the red plumage is a stain derived from a drop of blood that inflicted the bird when Roman soldiers thrust a sword into the side of the soon-to-be-crucified Christ (never mind that the grosbeak is only a new-world bird). We hang so many of our own projections—our own narratives and turgid symbolism—on birds, it's a wonder they can fly at all. But I don't mean to be completely dismissive of such mythmaking because, like the earliest human cave paintings of bulls and aurochs and bison, it can tell us something profound about our psychic connection to animals. My favorite bird myth comes from Papua New Guinea and involves the invention of music. A Kaluli boy and his sister were seining for crayfish. The sister caught some, but her brother did not. He begged his sister over and over for some of her crayfish, but she refused. At last, the boy grabbed a shrimp from the stream and pinched it over his nose until the flesh turned a reddish purple, the color of a muni bird's beak. His arms turned into wings, and the boy flew away. His sister begged him to come back, and she offered him some of her catch. But the flying boy replied in the falsetto cry of the muni bird, "Your crayfish you didn't give me. I have no sister."

The great American poet Nathaniel Mackey has interpreted this myth to mean that the source of music is what he calls the orphan's ordeal. In that context, music is at once "a complaint and a consolation." Out of the orphan's pain comes the salve of music. "Music," writes Mackey, "is wounded kinship's last resort." And the orphan's ordeal applies to any painful separation. When he lost Eurydice, Orpheus (whose very name haunts the word "orphan") turned that loss into music—music that simultaneously mourned and healed. Country music, the blues, the country-blues most of all—these keening art forms take loss as their fundamental subject and find a way to make that loss bearable. And the only way to make it bearable is to give it some kind of form. We can't *not* suffer, but we can give shape to that suffering, a shape that keeps us from drowning in the chaos. Christianity offers a *rationale* for why we suffer—we deserve to suffer for our ancestral disobedience in the garden—but it never overcomes the separation that is the cause of that suffering. It only offers an escape route out of this world—salvation through blood sacrifice. Music, by contrast, transforms our suffering and *reconciles us to the world once more*. Thus, while the song is initially a lament about broken kinship, it in the end becomes an articulation of homecoming. The bird, a symbol of flight, is also a symbol of the Orphic song that calls the animals back together. Pythagoras, said to be a student of Orpheus, promulgated the theory that music's harmonic laws echoed the laws of the *kosmos* (a term Pythagoras invented). Music, according to this theory, is the invisible syntax that binds the world's fragments back into a whole. It is a statement both of the disconnected *many* and the unified *one*. It affirms and justifies this life even in the midst of terrible suffering. It calls us *back* from the brink; it even makes the brink terribly beautiful.

The Stoics believed in a *pneuma* that was the "breath of life" by which the soul of God mingled with the soul of humans. Because music must ride the vibratory waves of the wind or breath, it becomes a physical manifestation of the *pneumatic world* we cannot see. This *pneuma* passing through a flute creates music, and we now know that *Homo sapiens* first made music by drilling five holes in the hollow wing bone of a griffin vulture, as if we have always suspected the connection between flight and song.

The iconoclastic musicologist Victor Zuckerkandl suggested that we should think about reality in terms of two interconnected worlds: the tangible, physical world and the invisible "tonal world"—the seen and the unseen. He argued that once we humans acquired speech, we used it to separate ourselves from the world all around us. We cast ourselves out of the garden.

In 1750, when the Puritan minister Jonathan Edwards began naming from his pulpit the "backsliders" of his own Northampton congregation, one of the condemned men committed suicide, and the church finally voted to dismiss Edwards. Contrast that sorry set of events with the sermon that Emily Dickinson imagined Orpheus preaching in a poem that begins with a survey of the Bible, "an antique volume" whose subject is "Sin—a distinguished Precipice." As if reflecting on Edwards's sermons and Zuckerkandl's theory of music, the poet observes, "Boys that 'believe' are very lonesome— / Other Boys are 'lost.'" Then she suggests another way to preach—through the birdlike, Orphic song:

> Had but the Tale a warbling Teller—
> All the Boys would come—
> Orpheus' Sermon captivated—
> It did not condemn—

In fact, it did the opposite—it unified all who came. Forty years later, in the third of his *Sonnets to Orpheus*, Rainer Maria Rilke restated Zuckerkandl's ontology this way: *Gesang is Dasein*—"song is reality" or "song is being." It's simple, says Rilke, for Orpheus. But for us, "our mind is split," split by the dualistic thinking that sets us apart from the world, that sets the ego apart from the other. "When can *we* be real?" asks the poet. The answer is when we let the music of self-expression turn into the music of self-effacement:

>   —learn
> To forget that passionate music. It will end.
> True singing is a different breath, about
> Nothing. A gust inside the god. A wind.

>   [tr. Stephen Mitchell]

In this last line, the tonal world of the *pneuma* breathes a new music into the physical body of the poet so that mere existence becomes true being. The world then becomes a work of art: reconciled, unified, even deified. When our speech achieved the wholeness of song, of music, then the speaker feels, as Rilke said, the breath of the god passing through the instrument of her body, and she will realize she is an emanation of, not an exile from, the world.

Ralph Waldo Emerson called language fossilized poetry because the language of philosophy, of theology, had lost the Stoic *pneuma* of inspiration, the rhythm of poetry. Once we humans acquired speech, we used it to separate ourselves from the world all around us. We *cast ourselves* out of the garden. Through poetry, tones return to our consciousness as the redemptive counterpart of words. They remind us through music that we belong here and that we can be reconciled to this realm if we elevate our thinking to the level of song—the medium that takes account of the world's twofold reality: *pneuma* and matter. In song, or in poetic speech, there is no split between subject and object, human-kind and the rest of the world. Song overcomes the ego of the subject that sees the rest of the world as a taxonomy of objects to be classified and judged. For the Stoics, the *pneuma*, like music, is the invisible syntax that unites the things it names. They are no longer individual objects but rather collective subjects—stars within the same constellation.

EARLY THIS MORNING on her way to work, Melissa dispatched me and my canoe onto Elkhorn Creek, about fifteen miles before its débouché into the Kentucky River. The creek drains five hundred acres of mostly farmland in the Inner Bluegrass and is the second-largest tributary of the Kentucky. After my father's death, my grandfather taught me to canoe throughout the inlets of the Chesapeake Bay, and that skill is at least one inheritance that came down to me uncomplicated. I remember the beautiful wood-and-canvas canoe my grandfather bought straight from the Old Town factory in the fifties. I had hoped that vessel at least would come down to me in the end as well, but instead he gave it to a member of his church. So instead, I paddle a twelve-foot, Old Town pack canoe that I bought myself and have owned for over twenty years. Made from light but durable composite materials, it is one of my most prized possessions and has never disappointed. This solo canoe is the essence of stream-lined simplicity, with one cane-bottom seat near the stern and one yoke across the beam. I can easily portage it through the northern Boundary Waters, glide across Umbagog Lake in Maine, even test its hull against class-three rapids on Kentucky's Rockcastle River.

But Elkhorn Creek is the perfect conduit for such a canoe, and I've been paddling this stretch since the eighties, essentially since I've had a driver's license to bring me here. In a vessel this small, one can feel overwhelmed by the size of the Kentucky River and the bass boats that careen up and down it. But measuring about fifty yards wide and a few feet deep in most places, the Elkhorn is suited only to motorless watercraft. Thus, with only my wooden, bent-shaft paddle, I ease my canoe out into the mainstream. Unlike the flat, slack water of the dammed Kentucky, the Elkhorn moves and is punctuated by riffles and small rapids that keep the trip interesting. I've packed along a jug of iced tea, two bologna sandwiches, and my fly rod. The sun is already shattering its silver light over the surface of the water, and the day feels promising indeed.

In "Song of Myself," this country's greatest poem, Walt Whitman imagines himself as "a Kentuckian walking the vale of the Elkhorn in my deer-skin leggings." For Whitman, this country was an emanation of his own expansive nature, and he saw himself as an embodiment of all its vast ecosystems. He felt no distinction between the land, with its vast circuitry of waterways, and his own flesh and blood; in my best moments, neither do I. Paddling these meanders, I can feel myself merge into this landscape and leave an anxious, defensive, self-enclosed ego behind. To be freed from the mind's churning cauldron and released into these more expansive elements feels like the very definition of liberation.

The Elkhorn's name comes either from the number of elk sheds that settlers found along its banks or from the notion that, seen from above, the meandering stream looks like the outlines of this ungulate's antlers. In *The Discovery, Settlement, and Present State of Kentucke*, the first book ever published about the state (my copy has the original typeface in which the letter *f* stands in for *s*), John Filson recounts that in 1754, one James McBride paddled down the Ohio River in a canoe, then "landed at the mouth of Kentucke river, and there marked a tree, with the firft letters of his name, and the date, which remain to this day." Not long after that, distillers began to settle beside the limestone-purified waters of the Elkhorn, inspiring Elijah Craig, a Baptist minister and hence the unlikely inventor of bourbon, to exclaim, "Heaven is a Kentucky of a place." In *The Discovery, Settlement, and Present State of Kentucke*, which among other things invented the myth of Daniel Boone, Filson tried to lure immigrants to the state with claims that its rivers and streams afforded abundant mill sites. A century later, Ebenezer Stedman bragged that his mill along the Elkhorn had produced "the first Sheet of paper in the Great West." Unfortunately, Stedman ran afoul of his pro-Union neighbors when he provided the secessionist government of Jefferson Davis (unfortunately born in Kentucky) with badly needed paper on which to print Confederate money. But Filson continued to perpetuate the notion of Kentucky as a second Eden, and he argued that the bottomlands throughout the Inner Bluegrass were some of the richest soils in the country. He said this landscape is characterized by "small rifings, and declivities, which form a beautiful profpect."

Such a prospect is still on display today as this karst terrain undulates away from Elkhorn Creek. Water maples, sycamore, and hackberry trees lean long and low over the water from both banks, writing their reflections onto its still surface. Red-winged blackbirds and various species of flycatchers rove the air along the banks. Painted turtles sun on deadfalls, and they drop into the water only reluctantly when I steer too close.

After a sedentary gray winter, the paddle feels once more like it belongs in my hands as I J-stroke out into the middle of the creek. For me, guiding a canoe has become an act so elemental to being human that time itself seems to vanish, and this present is measured only by each stroke of my paddle. It becomes a kind of meditation, where paying attention to each stroke bears some resemblance to the Buddhist on her zafu, consciously gauging each breath. The point for both, it seems to me, is to inhabit the moment, the present, completely. There is no hurry and no place to be but here. In his beautiful book, *The Singing Wilderness*, Sigurd Olson writes that when a man settles into a canoe, "he feels at last that he is down to the real business of living." I agree completely. What's more, I am deliberately following my genetic lineage back to the hunters and gatherers who wandered these woods and fields twelve thousand years ago. They weren't builders of civilizations, and they left few artifacts behind—just some flint spear points and chert tools. They gathered walnuts and hunted mastodons in small, roving bands. They paddled dugout canoes, probably fashioned from the straight, soft wood of tulip poplars, and collected mussels on the Elkhorn's shoals. And while the materials have changed, the form and function of the modern canoe has seen little innovation, nor is any needed. I could travel back farther still, all the way to my species' watery origins. There, the canoe becomes a sleek fish, while I am its pumping heart, my paddle blade its tail fin. I would become submerged into an earlier, antediluvian kinship with all other species.

As the creek follows its elkhorn-like contours, limestone palisades rise up along the outer banks. I stop paddling, quickly rig up my fly rod with a Clouser Minnow, and start casting into shadows at the base of the bluffs. When things are going well, this fly rod feels as much like a natural extension of my arm as does my paddle. But after a winter off, my casting is rusty, and it takes a while to find the fluid rhythms that make good anglers look like orchestra conductors leading the string section through a slow movement. After a few minutes, a smallmouth is wriggling at the end of my line. Its bronze flanks flash in the sun as I excise the hook and watch the fish slap out of my hand, back into the cool water.

Paddling again, I tack left and right across the current, looking for the deepest troughs through the riffles and rapids. At one cutback, I duck low to miss a sycamore branch hanging at eye level. My forehead brushes against an old, tattered prayer flag still dangling from the branch. Up on the bank, two geese are standing perfectly still, watching this strange man-fish splash pass them. When the current finally shoots me out of a bouncing wave train, I decide to drift over to a shaded rock bar for lunch.

As I sit on a fallen tree trunk, eating my sandwiches, I notice the jawbone of a deer lying among the cobble at my feet. Matted in the mud just beyond it is the slightly sinister skull and skeleton of a longnose gar. In his book *Elkhorn: Evolution of a Kentucky Landscape*, former state poet laureate Richard Taylor tells the story of William Hutcherson, who in 1945 was bulldozing nearby land for a stock pond when he unearthed bones far too large for any animal he had ever seen. He called up state geologist Willard Jillson, who confirmed that Hutcherson had discovered the tusks, vertebrae, and skull of a Columbian mammoth. Thirteen feet tall at the shoulders and weighing close to ten tons, the Pleistocene mammoth would have entered North American from Asia about 1.5 million years ago, along with mastodons and giant ground sloths. The mammoth, whose bones were perhaps fifty thousand years old, would have lived here until the last glacial retreat twelve thousand years ago. In this country, we have grown so used to smaller, docile mammals since we drove all the larger ones to extinction. Now it's hard to conceive of an elephant-like creature, with deadly ivory tusks longer than a man, coming down to this very bank to drink. But it would be a miraculous thing to see. Nature red in tooth and tusk, not tamed by distilleries and dams.

Back in my canoe, I glide through deeper pools, where large northern drum drift slowly beneath my hull. A red-horse swims by with a huge chunk gouged out of its tail. Further on, a green heron fishes the shallows while I shoot out my own monofilament line, this time in vain. The day has grown too hot for the smallmouth to bother with my lures, so I put my rod away and return to the repetitive pleasure of carving the letter *J* onto the surface of the water and moving at the pace of close, quiet observation. As I pass under a concrete bridge, cliff swallows scatter. At the top of one pylon, they are busy building their complex of mud nests that look like a dozen small earthenware jugs turned on their sides and molded together. It's a fascinating feat of architecture, with the "mouth" of each jug just large enough for a single swallow to poke out its head and scan for insects. The swallows return to their perches as soon as I'm gone.

I wind on past farms and fisheries, old black tobacco barns and abandoned home sites. Overhead, two hawks carve an invisible Venn diagram into the air. To take in all of these various fish and fowl is to find oneself inured, if only for a while, from all of the urban distractions and responsibilities that wait just beyond the banks of Elkhorn Creek. It's a bit deflating, then, to see in the distance the overpass for State Road 127, under which I parked my truck this morning. In such moments, I often think of the Brian Wilson song "I Just Wasn't Made for These Times." In fact, as I watch many of the things I love most disappear—books, newspapers, record stores, wild animals, and wild places—I feel Wilson's sentiment more and more frequently, more and more despondently. Last summer, when I was riding horseback through the Rockies in Montana on my way to fish the Flathead River, I had an overwhelming impression that *this is the proper way to see the country*—on a narrow horse trail with no car or highway in sight. Now I think the same thing as I follow this even older, natural highway that would lead me down to the Kentucky River, then the Ohio and the Mississippi, and finally to the Gulf of Mexico, if I let it.

PULL THE GODS out of the sky. Put them back in the woods. Now we are getting somewhere.

I AM LYING in the grass beneath our ash trees, watching the red-bellied woodpeckers, these spear-headed javelins, throw themselves into freefalls out of which they rise only at the last moment, inches from the ground. I have listened to their percussive drumming all morning. Here at Clear Creek, I have seen (almost daily) every woodpecker that inhabits the eastern woods: hairy, downy, red-headed, red-bellied, pileated, yellow-bellied sapsucker, and the northern flicker. Indeed, *Picidae* might be the most important bird family in this small watershed. With their hammering heads, the woodpeckers create nesting sites for a host of other birds, owls, bats, and flying squirrels. Down in the bottom, dead box elders are riddled with woodpecker holes that have created an entire habitat—a sort of woodland high-rise—for a diverse community of forest dwellers. And in fact, some of the woodpeckers have (understandably, I suppose) mistaken our cedar-sided house for a tree. It began when carpenter bees burrowed into the eaves and the wood siding. They made perfect quarter-inch holes in which the females laid eggs. Then red-bellies came to feed on the eggs and in the process made much larger holes. Then families of squirrels moved through those openings and set up house between the cedar and interior drywall. In the early morning, we heard them tumbling around inside the walls as if training for the circus. Having soon had enough of that, I climbed up my extension ladder, convinced the squirrels that they really needed to relocate, and replaced the siding.

Still, I like the idea of thinking of the house *as* a tree. That started a few weeks ago, when two brothers with the Moses Drilling Company pulled their enormous truck into our driveway. They were here to tap into the volcanic heat that lay 150 feet below my house. The Moses's drill itself rose from the back of the truck until it stood perpendicular to the massive flatbed. Then the roaring top head began to slowly bore into the limestone substrate beneath my gravel driveway. The drill itself hung in thirty-foot intervals from a winch that slowly spun like the cylinder inside a revolver. Each time one section drilled down thirty feet, the cylinder turned, and one of the Moses brothers attached another section to the drill until the borehole reached down 150 feet. They drilled two more such holes, then snaked down into each two long, thin pipes that, when attached to a geothermal heat pump in my basement, will heat and cool our house with the solar energy trapped in all of that limestone.

"This stuff would be good on your garden," one of the Moses brothers said to me, gesturing to a mound of the pulverized white limestone. And I realized he was right; it would indeed raise the soil pH. So while the brothers backfilled the holes with gravel, I filled my wheelbarrow with loads of this gray powder. As I spread it over my raised beds, I kept thinking: what I'm holding in my shovel, with the weight and consistency of flour, is five-hundred-million-year-old sedimentary rock. That's how long it lay buried beneath the garden, where it would now slowly sink back into the topsoil, replacing nutrients as it did.

As for my house-as-tree metaphor, it would go something like this: The cedar siding is its insulating bark, the new geothermal tubes will pull heat from the ground as if they were its roots, and the solar shingles I plan to eventually install will be its leaves. These last two will transfer energy in the same way water travels up a tree's microscopic phloem tubes and gets photosynthesized by leaves into sugars that are then carried back down through the tree's xylem tubes. The garden, which I think of as an extension of the house, will nourish the large mammals—us—that live inside it. Finally, the large wooden beams that run throughout the interior of the house are sequestering carbon, as does a tree. It's not a perfect analogy, I admit, but the point is I want our house, like a tree, to thrive on recurring sources of energy: the sun, the soil, the substrate, the water that powers the Mother Ann Lee Hydroelectric Plant that electrifies our house, and the trees that have died around it, providing firewood. I want our house to be integrated into this steep slope ecosystem, not set off from it. I want our house to look like it has made an effort to belong here—unobtrusively, respectfully, in flattering imitation of the woods that surround it.

MANY YEARS AGO, I decided to create my own "bible" with a pair of scissors. I did not, like Thomas Jefferson, simply excise the miracles from the Gospels of the New Testament. Rather, I began xeroxing passages from writers who seemed vital to me at the time: Whitman, Heraclitus, Dickinson, Thoreau, Rilke, Nietzsche, Muriel Rukeyser, Jean Toomer, Hafiz, Blake, D. T. Suzuki, Lao Tzu, the Gospel of Thomas, and many others. I clipped out those passages and pasted them randomly into a blank artist's sketchbook, intentionally avoiding any attestation for each passage. I also added images I had clipped from seed catalogs, along with inept watercolor scenes I painted around some passages. My plan was for each writer's words to blend into the others until what emerged was one collective voice of instruction and inspiration. I wrote an introductory poem that began: "A book written with scissors / discerned through distillation . . ." And it worked. Now, when I pull this collage text down from the shelf and read it some mornings, I often no longer remember who said what, only that it was said and it moved me at an earlier time in my life. For instance, I read this morning: "The gods are of no sect; they side with no man." I don't remember who said that, only that it was said. I could, of course, look it up on the internet, but that would defeat the purpose of my project. The polyphony has now merged into one voice, one scripture that speaks to me and only to me (in fact, no one else knows this "book" exists, though I never meant to keep it a secret). Whatever writerly ego went into producing the original texts has been cauterized. The many selves behind these passages have faded, and only the beauty of the words and the thoughts remain. It's as if a collection of individual trees has become a forest, a single organism. Emerson wrote that every religion should have a congregation of one. I believe that. And this is that congregation's hymnal—a bit worn but still a reassuring presence there in the pew, a comforting thing to pick up some incidental Sabbath day.

THE CREEK IS a good companion: that's what I think each day as I walk along its banks, tripping over sycamore roots, sometimes swinging from wild grape vines when my mind grows expansive. In my peripheral vision, I register the unmistakable blue flash of an indigo bunting as it flits through the spicebush, whose leaves give off a lemony fragrance when rubbed between my hands. The narrow trail rises and falls as it follows the outline of the creek's eastern bank. Though my morning routine down by the creek varies little—coffee, reading, writing, watching—I do make it a practice to move up and down the bank with my portable office. Today, I'm sitting in one of my favorite spots beside a bend in the creek where the water quickens and whitens briefly around a thick receding strata of limestone. With what looks like methodical moroseness, a blackbird walks and pokes at the stones along the waterline as if it has lost something of great value there. Orioles dart back and forth across the creek as if they were running cable for some invisible hanging bridge, maybe a bridge of sighs for the blackbird. This is a frequent fishing spot for a great blue heron, who right now is standing as still as a stick, perhaps because he has spotted me but more likely because he is trying to convince the sunfish and stonerollers that he *is* a stick, an innocuous piece of the landscape. At times, he swings his anvil of a head around on his snake of a neck. Then he resumes his stick pose.

I unfold my chair on a flat boulder that's almost exactly the size and shape of a casket and that sits slightly apart from the bank like its own small island. All around the rock, in the three feet of quiet water, a small school of creek chubs hover, absolutely still. They all point in the same direction and look as if they are waiting, in perfect equipoise, to begin some race upstream. Even when I accidentally kick a stone into the water, they barely flinch. A smallmouth bass darts beneath them, rolling quickly to flash its silvery keel. This half-a-billion-year-old island rock is covered with a kind of bas-relief carved by the waters that are now flowing around me. These vaguely creature-like glyphs make up an alphabet I can't decipher, a language lost to me, though sometimes the water coming over the riffle a hundred feet upstream does sound, just for an instant, like a human voice. But then it reverts again to its own native tongue. I wonder, Could I teach myself the language written in this stone or the one spoken by the rushing water? It's a question that called me to Clear Creek in the first place—a question that brought me to dwell in the woods above this gorge. Which is really just to say, I wanted to learn the language of belonging. The more I can identify trees, flowers, fish, birdsongs, the more I come into their company, the more I feel that I have *earned* their company. The French poet Stéphane Mallarmé said that to name something is to kill it, and I know what he means. What's more, language betrays us, becomes most tenuous, at exactly those times when we want it to accomplish the most—with a word like "being" for another example, or "spirit." Language, it seems to me, simply isn't at home in such abstraction. It wants to *name* something concrete: flint, lobelia, bullfrog. In that way, I think, it calls us into the specific, into a particular place, and therefore helps us more fully inhabit that moment. That is to say, it calls us into the present (time) of presence (place). In that sense, naming is the opposite of killing something. Rather, naming—true naming, poetic naming—calls a thing closer, as if in a kind of secular prayer. It calls the subjective namer and the objective thing, say a chinquapin oak, into the orbit of the other so that subject and object are no longer distinctive but part of a shared experience. The ego-limited "I" expands into something larger. The breath, the *pneuma* of the namer, commingles with the breath, the oxygen, that the tree emits. And in this way, they call each other back into a symbolic belonging.

But what estranged us in the first place? The pre-Socratic philosopher Heraclitus said, "The Logos is eternal but men have not heard it and men have heard it and not understood. . . . One must talk about everything according to its nature, how it comes to be and how it grows. Men have talked about the world without paying attention to the world or to their own minds, as if they were asleep or absent-minded." Men and women have simply not paid enough attention to nature or to their human nature. Thus, we have explained ourselves away from the world. What exactly does Heraclitus mean by the Logos? His most faithful modern student, the German philosopher Martin Heidegger, translates the Heraclitean Logos as "the primal gathering principle" in nature. It is the "intrinsic togetherness" of being itself. It is, one might say, the original law of ecology that binds into a whole what the ancient Chinese poets called the ten thousand things. Of course, now we know it's more like ten million species, but the same ecological law of the Logos still applies. The great mistake that the Greeks after Heraclitus made was to turn this law of nature into a linguistic abstraction; they reduced the Logos to mere logic. Plato wanted to lead us out of the cave of the world into the light of abstract truth. But Heraclitus would have said, "You are talking about the world without paying attention to it." He would have said, "This cave is actually pretty interesting. Look, for instance, at those impressive paintings of bison, aurochs, and reindeer on the walls. Look at the fossils under your feet. This cave suits me just fine." Plato desperately wanted to find a philosophy—a language—that might lead him out of the cave. But contemporary Heraclitean philosophers like John Dewey, Ludwig Wittgenstein, and Richard Rorty said that's simply not the point of language. Language doesn't have the capacity to encapsulate the truth; hence, no culture can ever agree on a definition. The point of language is to operate *in* the cave—in this world. It is to be a pragmatic tool of human use—a way to solve problems that arise inside the cave.

But of course, Plato won the day, and Western peoples have been trying to escape the cave ever since. Tellingly, Heidegger suggested that this devolution into logic occurred when the Logos moved indoors, when it became "an affair of schools." Epicurus had taught in a garden, the Stoics in an outdoor portico. But in the indoor philosophy schools that followed, curriculum killed the Logos.

We might even say the same thing about the radical shift from the outdoor teachings of a Mediterranean wanderer named Yeshua to the churches of the Apostle Paul. Pauline Christianity in particular cottoned on to Platonic philosophy because it too wanted to find an eternal truth outside this temporal world. By the time that religion reached the New World and formed the Massachusetts Bay Colony, the marriage of abstract language and fear of the Heraclitean world had reached a shrill crescendo. The Puritans spoke and wrote in grand abstractions. "Providence" had brought them here to smite the godless "heathens" that lurked in the darkness around their "Everlasting Light," according to Increase Mather. The Puritans feared this world and yearned for the next. I only mention them to bring things back to native soil and because they seem the starkest example of what I'm talking about—an estrangement from and a denigration of the world, paired with a substitution of abstract human logic for biology's primal Logos.

Which brings me back to naming. In the 1920s, when Anglo poetry was replete with vague and florid language, Ezra Pound urged American and British literature onto a new tack. Drunk on the highly imagistic, stripped-down syntax of ancient Chinese poetry, he invented a movement called Imagism. The Chinese language, of course, consists of pictographic ideograms: the symbol looks like the thing it represents. Pound couldn't invent a new alphabet, but he could try to make English poetry as concrete as possible, eschewing rhetorical flourishes and tacked-on meanings. The poem would simply stand as sturdy or as ephemeral as the scene it represented. And in doing so, it would pull the reader back into a more immediate connection to the natural world. We would pass through the images of the poem back into our own experience of the real. The invisible Logos could do the rest.

Speaking of which, consider a poem I just found this morning, left in an abandoned robin's nest by the Reclusive Socialist:

The Unnamable
that can be named
is not the Unnamable.

One should speak
of only what one can:

the stone rollers nosing pebbles
along the creek bottom,
for instance.

That's why I like a poem
with a lot of emptiness
around it,

a lot of space left
for the things
that can't be said,

                    or that are said
                    in silence

by the Unnamable,
speaking its presence,

which we take
through our inattention

                    for absence.

I think I see what he's trying to do here. The first lines, if I'm not mistaken, are a rough translation of the first stanza of the *Tao Te Ching*. And it certainly feels and looks like he was trying to write a Chinese poem, spare and lean. That line about "our inattention" certainly sounds like Heraclitus. As for the Unnamable, I think the Reclusive Socialist is saying that what we call God is at once everywhere and nowhere— so elusive because this force exists in the one place we never thought to look, right in front of us.

I fold up the poem and put it in my pocket. Just upstream, the creek continues its own everlasting dive through the riffles in a rushing tumble. After I write that sentence, I look back at it, and because I've been thinking about language all morning, I vaguely remember a linguistic theory that says all language originated from humans trying to imitate the sounds of nature. That theory certainly finds no better evidence than moving water. *Riffle, rushing, runnel, tumble*: all words that sound like what they mean to describe. Then there's *murmur, gurgle, babble, guzzle*. When humans invented writing, such onomatopoetics found their visual equivalent in the Chinese pictograph, the letter that looks like the thing itself. Western alphabets flirted with pictorial writing through cuneiform and hieroglyphics but soon abandoned it because some smart person realized that there were only so many sounds the human voice could make. Therefore, an alphabet based on sound instead of image would be immanently simpler and easier to execute. Today, English words and letters on the page no longer look anything like the things they are meant to represent (except

perhaps for the capital Q, a monkey with its tail dangling).
Some linguists see this break from visual representation as
a loss, a rupture with the natural world. The argument goes
that when our language became detached from nature, so
did we. Our abstract alphabet allowed us to treat the natural world as an abstraction, a "resource" to be used and
abused. It is true, as Ezra Pound discovered, that the first
poetry devoted to the natural world originated in the most
imagistic language, Chinese. Just think of the pictographic
poems written by Wang Wei (707–761 CE) in the margins of
his beautiful landscape paintings. But under Mao Zedong,
the Chinese abused and polluted the natural world with the
same willful abandon as an Appalachian strip mine opera-
tor, and today, the air in Beijing isn't fit to breathe. What's
more, it's conceivable that our nonpictographic alphabet actually makes the brain's limbic system work harder, and thus
more successfully, to conjure natural images. Consider the
word *jewelweed* (I'm considering it because the actual flower
is growing up on the bank near where I'm sitting). Even if
one doesn't know what jewelweed looks like, the word itself
is evocative, sonorous. It's a beautiful combination of conso-
nance and assonance. What we lose in image gets made up
for in sound. And its image is still implied in the word—it
creates a mental image of some sort of grass that glitters in
some way. It still has the potential to call us off the page of
the poem and into the watershed where jewelweed grows. It
pulls us back into the original poem of creation and reminds
us that the Judeo-Christian God, Yahweh, *called* the world
into being. In the beginning was the Word.

AT THE FAR end of my neighbor's field, where the woods
draw a curtain across the moonless dark, lightning bugs are
beginning to create momentary, frenetic constellations
inside the trees. One constellation flashes for an instant,
then disappears, only to reemerge in some other configura-
tion. At the top of the tree line, all of this flickering light
stops and gives way to the more enduring glow of the stars.
These lower constellations know nothing of eternities; those
upper constellations know nothing of the moment.

IT'S BLACKBERRY WINTER, a late spring cold snap, and I'm
sitting in the garden in a flannel shirt with my coffee and
notebook. One raised bed is filled with spinach and lettuce,
while another corrals broccoli, brussels sprouts, kale, and
six-feet-tall snap peas whose white blossoms sway in the
light breeze. Cucumbers are sprouting from their mounds,
and the caged tomatoes are almost two feet high. I set my
tallest plants on the north side of the garden so they wouldn't
shade the smaller ones and so I can peruse the whole operation from my chair thirty feet away on the south side of the
beds. From this seat, I can admire the sturdiness of the broccoli stalks, the texture of the kale, the opportunistic tendrils
of the snap peas. It's calming to sit here among this leafy
profusion. I can feel my heart rate slow and my mind settle.
The reason, I think, is one I've already alluded to: the human
mind exists in such sympathy with the natural world because
it evolved to do so. The city is such a recent invention that the
mind struggles to make sense of it. And when the mind can't
make sense, it often becomes anxious, depressed, violent. So
anyone in New York who can afford to buys a condo within

sight of Central Park. A few years ago, less well-to-do New Yorkers started unrolling Astroturf in curbside parking spaces, where they then plopped down lawn chairs and fed the meter all day in exchange for that makeshift pastoral. I'm not saying they all wanted to go charging back to the Pleistocene; I'm saying they were comically desperate to bring even the verisimilitude of nature back into their lives.

The irony of this—an irony I'm reminded of constantly—is that most New Yorkers drive far less than I do and consequently burn less fossil fuel. Indeed, the chief virtue of any city is that, if rightly designed, it allows one to walk, bike, or take public transportation to work, school, restaurants, shops, and beyond. Density and condensity are what recommend urban living and what should reduce city dwellers' carbon footprint. Because it pains me to think that someone living in downtown Lexington, surrounded by buildings and shopping at the farmers' market, might be a better environmentalist than me living in my vernal seclusion, I've tried to practice a certain amount of self-sufficiency that translates into fewer trips to the store and shortened supply lines to the resources I do need.

Last night for dinner, we ate lamb chops from nearby Lanes Landing Farm, along with snap peas and a spinach salad from our garden. We ate out under the locust trees, where a pair of goldfinches picked thistle from the feeders.

All of this modest pleasure put me in mind of Epicurus, the garden-philosopher who lived 2,300 years ago, and who said the achievement of pleasure and happiness, along with the avoidance of fear and pain, are the aims of life and the aims of philosophy. Indeed, for Epicurus (like Thoreau), philosophy was not something one *thinks* but something one *does*. Of Epicurus's three hundred papyrus scrolls, with titles like *On Nature* and *On the Gods*, only three letters and a collection of aphorisms have survived. As a result, a person can read all of Epicurus in an evening, and that's what I planned to do. And since Epicurus founded his school in a house and garden on the outskirts of Athens, I took my slim volume up to my own vegetable garden, settled into a very weathered Adirondack chair, and turned to the "Letter to Menoeceus."

It contains an impressive and concise statement of the Epicurean principles. The gods exist, writes Epicurus, but far away in another realm where they harbor absolutely no interest in the human drama unfolding on our tiny planet. We should neither fear nor invent superstitious notions about them. From there, it follows that we should not fear death either. As if addressing the cult of Christianity invented by the Apostle Paul—not the wandering teacher named Yeshua—Epicurus writes that the fear of death and the consequent desire for immortality prevents us from truly attaining happiness in this world. So does the fear of not knowing what follows this life. The Epicurean solution to this cuts like Occam's razor: death should mean nothing to us since "while we exist, death is not present, and whenever death is present, we do not exist." By rejecting the fear of death, Epicurus returns our attention to *this* life, whereas Pauline Christianity did the exact opposite. Indeed, I have often wondered, If the fear of death and the promise of life after death were removed from mainstream Christianity, how compelled would modern American Christians be to follow the teachings of, say, the Sermon on the Mount? The vast majority don't seem compelled to follow those teachings even now.

Once Epicurus dispels the fear of gods and death, he turns to the question of how we should live here and now. Like few philosophers before or after him, he says we should live happily. Happiness derives from two things: health of the body and calmness of the soul, and true pleasure means "freedom from bodily pain and mental anguish." Epicureanism is not hedonism, as is often thought. Wine is good; drunkenness and liver disease are not. A pleasure that eventually leads to pain (liver disease) or to the wounding of others (adultery, say) is not a true pleasure, writes Epicurus, and so we should "pass over many pleasures, whenever greater difficulty follows from them." The truest pleasures, he says, can be found in a self-sufficient modesty because modesty doesn't lead to insatiable cravings that make happiness ever elusive, nor does it lead to a depressing level of debt. We Americans, for example, consume twice as much materially than we did forty years ago, yet all psychological indicators show we are no happier for it. Epicurus's maxim on what we now call consumerism goes like this: "Everything easy to procure is natural while everything difficult to obtain is superfluous. Plain dishes offer the same pleasure as a luxurious table, when the pain that comes from want is taken away." There is something immanently sensible about this formula, and it reminds me of Walt Whitman's bitter passage in *Leaves of Grass* where he writes that he might "turn and live with the animals" since "not one of them is demented with the mania of owning things." That, for Epicurus, is

the all-too-human mania that leads to an unhappiness unknown in the rest of the natural world. As a consequence,
Epicurus believed that the study of nature would make us
more modest and self-sufficient. Rather than using the resources of the natural world five times faster than they can
be replenished—as we do now—we would learn the lessons
of, say, a watershed. A natural watershed, after all, with its
geographical boundaries, is by its very nature self-sufficient.
It circulates its own wealth over and over. It generates no
waste and does not "externalize" the cost of "production"
onto other streams and valleys. In a watershed, *all* energy is
renewable and all resource use is sustainable. The watershed
purifies air and water, holds soil in place, enriches humus,
and sequesters carbon. That is to say, a watershed economy
improves the land and thus improves the lives of the people
who inhabit that particular place. It is an economy based
not on the unsustainable, shortsighted logic of never-end-
ing *growth*, which robs the future to meet the needs of the
present, but rather on maintaining the health, well-being,
and stability of the human and the land community. The accumulation economy of the United States, which consumes
25 percent of the planet's resources for an insatiable 5 percent of its population, clearly violates Epicurus's definition
of pleasure as something that must not cause the current suffering of the world's poor and the future suffering of our descendants. That, says Epicurus, is an injustice, and there can
be no true happiness where injustice exists. Though the execution of justice changes with the circumstances, Epicurus
writes that "justice is the same for all, because it is a kind
of mutual benefit in men's interactions with one another."

Occam's razor again: justice is societal, a pact not to harm or be harmed. Justice is a pragmatic attempt to maximize the pleasure of all, not a predatory hoarding that creates intolerable suffering and inequality.

I put my book down and stared out across my raised beds, cogitating. Whoever Menoeceus was, that was one hell of a letter he received around 290 BCE. Rereading it now, I realize how sensibly and directly it speaks to the anxieties and inadequacies of twenty-first-century America. It asks us to shift our definitions of happiness away from unsustainable consumption toward more fundamental sources: friends, family, and the natural world. It tells us that more modest consumption will lead to more justice for all—especially for the Asian poor who make so much of what we consume. It tells us that virtue and happiness are not inconsistent, nor are happiness and justice. It tells us we are right to want parks and gardens in cities—especially in cities—so we can reclaim a part of our genetic past that will make us more fully human.

THE WORLD: A self-creating god.

THIS MORNING, JIM KRUPA comes out to help me do an inventory of the fish in Clear Creek. He and I are splashing through a shallower section with a four-by-six-foot seine stretched between two wooden poles. We dip the seine into a foot of water and catch a few young sunfish that look like flat green stones the creek has been polishing for a million years. They still seem coeval with these other rocks that were once the bones of brachiopods and sea lilies, pressed between pages in this book of waves. Their sides are a deep green, speckled with flecks of blue that look like they have been borrowed from the sky. We hold them in our wet palms, where they flash in the sunlight—promising auguries, I think, for a good year on a good creek.

Then Jim says, "Hold up. Look at that stick."

I gaze down into the foot-deep water at a brown, fallen branch. Except it isn't a dead branch. We sweep the seine up under it, and when we pop the wooden stretchers out of the water, a two-foot longnose gar is thrashing in the net. It had simply been lying in wait for insects, crustaceans, and smaller fish. It certainly hadn't reckoned on two hominids with a large net splashing by.

Jim, who is fearless, grabs *Lepisosteus osseus* (meaning "bony" and "scale" in Latin) by its snout and caudal region. The glittering, interlocking scales are olivaceous, and there are dark spots along its sides and tail fin. The scales look like a sleek suit of armor. But if you do cut down through that armor, Jim assures me that the meat is actually pretty good. The desperate settlers at Jamestown dined on quite a lot of longnose gar four hundred years ago. Jim sets the antediluvial fish back down in the water, and it quickly thrashes away. A few yards upstream, among some submerged rocks, we net a small school of golden redhorse, named, I surmise, for their crimson fins. Then we wrangle a foot-long northern drum, whose purplish dorsal fin runs the length of its body and who seems to have been trapped in this shallow pool by the recent lack of rain. Further upstream, we catch striped, emerald, and river shiners, blunt-nose minnows,

white suckers, spotted bass, smallmouth bass, green-sided and rainbow darters, creek chubs, and hog-suckers.

I ask Jim what he thinks of Clear Creek's health and diversity. He says a rock-bottom stream like this never has quite as many species as one where the fish can feed, hide, and build nests in a mud bottom. But the main thing that troubles him is we haven't netted any stonerollers.

"In a creek this size, they should be here."

Then we stretch the seine across a narrow rill and snap it up to find a writhing school of stonerollers. I pick up one of these Sisyphus-like minnows to examine the rounded snout with which it rolls pebbles into a mounded nest.

A little further upstream, in quieter water, we come upon a colony of longear sunfish. My shadow scatters the fish for a moment, but soon they are back, darting around three nests the males built out of creek gravel. Sunfish practice lek

mating; that is, males gather as a group to compete for females, a human beauty pageant in reverse. The bellies of the
males are bright orange, while an iridescent blue mottling
spreads from the mouth, down along the sides and through
the dorsal fins. With those fins fully extended, the male sunfish swims close to the female and flashes his seasonal opu-
lence. She will choose the most beautiful male; then, back
at his nest, spawning will commence. Female sunfish are
polyandrous, so the male will look after the eggs. But for
the moment, this is her guy, and this is natural selection in
its most obvious execution. As for a less spectacular male,
the *sneaker* (that's actually the scientific term) will practice
his own evolutionary adaptation: he will attempt to infil-
trate the nest of the presumably distracted spawning pair
and drop in some sperm of his own. When the female has
finished laying her eggs, as many as two thousand, she will
vanish downstream to find a new colony of potential suitors.
The male stays to tend his hearth, dusting the nest with his
tail to keep out debris. And he'll keep at it until the larvae
have hatched. Thus, Darwin's theory of evolution ensures
that the most potentially dazzling sunfish will inherit Clear
Creek.

Today, evolutionary biologists argue about whether this
is sexual selection or natural selection at work. In what way,
after all, does the beauty of the male sunfish serve future
sunfish? If anything, it might make them more vulnera-
ble to predators. Some have said it shows his overall health
as a breeder—good color means good genes—and this is
what attracts the female. Or maybe, as Darwin believed,
the female sunfish is simply attracted to the male for his

ostensible beauty. In this view, beauty doesn't need a utilitarian function: the female likes what she likes and she is capable, like a human, of appreciating that beauty. Some biologists find this notion that a fish has an actual aesthetic far too anthropocentric. But you could argue the opposite: that it is anthropocentric to think *only* humans can appreciate outward beauty. Either way, it does raise the question, What *is* the use of beauty—for any animal? Obviously, beautiful people, like beautiful sunfish, tend to get what they want more often than others. And what they want, first and foremost, is recognition. They want to be *seen* as beautiful. After all, without the perceiver of the beautiful, beauty is worthless. Of course, like the male sunfish, they want this recognition to lead to something else—namely success, whether we want to define that in terms of sex, acceptability, affluence, power, or lineage. Though he doesn't know it, the male sunfish wants above all else to get his genes into the next generation, and he'll take great evolutionary risks to do so. That is, he'll evolve ostentatious traits that seem obviously detrimental to his survival, except that he gets the girl. Because the female prefers a beautiful male, beauty becomes an evolutionary trait, and sexual selection becomes a kind of natural selection. Thus, beauty is in some way evolutionary—a means to an end.

Whatever the case, in all of his useful or useless beauty, the longear sunfish seems perfectly adapted to this clear, shallow water. But what of the other aqueous animals that were not? One bomb evolutionary biologists like to drop on creationists is that 99 percent of all species that ever lived have gone extinct. Why would an intelligent designer ever let that happen, or why would he—the creationists all agree on ID's gender—design so poorly in the first place? It's a good retort, but it shares the same assumptions as those of the creationists: namely, that because the creator is divine by his very nature, then he must be perfect, and therefore, his creation must be as well. But why? To show that the god of monotheism is better than the gods of the Greeks or the Hindus? Perhaps, but based on all of the biological evidence, I find it far easier to believe in a god who more resembles an artist as *we* understand him or her. Art may be very beautiful, but it doesn't have to be perfect, and it doesn't have to be perfect—whatever that might mean—to be beautiful. "There is no reason," wrote evolutionary biologist Jerry Coyne, "why a celestial designer, fashioning organisms from scratch like an architect designs buildings, should make new species by remodeling the features of existing ones." Coyne seems here to fall into the creationists' trap of assuming he can know the mind of a creator. That is to say, he leaves the scientific realm for the theological, a realm where science supposedly doesn't tread. But as to his assertion that a celestial designer would never create organisms from existing organisms, one must ask, why not? It's the way a jazz musician works, after all, improvising on what has come before. In an excellent essay "The Imperfect Art," music historian Ted Gioia argues that jazz is an imperfect medium specifically because it is based on improvisation and spontaneity. The genius of a jazz musician rests almost singularly on his or her ability to improvise a solo. We prize great jazz soloists because, like nature, they are inventing in real time, with no chance of revision. Everything must move forward, right or wrong, and everything depends on what has come before—invention growing out of tradition. And architecture itself is obviously based on past designs; no architect works "from scratch." Adaptation is as much an artistic drive as it is an evolutionary one. Indeed, art is an endless reworking of what has come before. And a lot of that reworking doesn't work: an artist was trying something new and it just didn't succeed for whatever reason. Back to the canvas, the page, the trumpet, the species.

It bothers me not at all to believe in a less-than-perfect original artist who created an astonishing, if flawed, world. Except in my own Stoic conception of the world, the artist *is* the art. Spinoza's God-or-Nature is a poem that writes itself: an endless improvisation. However imperfect. Still beautiful.

I MUST HAVE come close to an oriole nest as I walked to the creek today because the male grew agitated as I passed by, and he started shooting from tree to tree, issuing a low rattling call of distress. Down on my small, Ordovician island rock, blues flitter from one piece of raccoon scat to another. I watch barn swallows chase each other up and down the creek with incredible velocity and torque. As on most days, I have the creek to myself. For a while now, I have begun to feel my life growing narrower here in the woods, less peopled but also less distracted. Living on Clear Creek, solitude has increasingly become my companion. I certainly spend far more time alone than I ever have in my life. Melissa goes to work during the day, and I'm now too far from town to just hop in for lunch with a friend or go casually browse through a record store or bookstore (and anyway, the last two independent record and bookstores closed this year). I drive in to teach two days a week, but other than that, it's mostly me and Clear Creek.

I think my desire for solitude is in part genetic. My ancestors were Norwegian. They lived in a sparsely populated country with long winters that isolated them further from each other. As a result, Norwegians developed a "one man, one mountain" mentality. Self-reliance and the ability to draw on inner resources were essential. As an American child, I spent a lot of time alone—drawing, reading, wandering—and I appreciate that my parents allowed me that space and time to do as I pleased. Many afternoons, I would walk to the recently closed high school down the street and kick field goals on the empty football field. My adopted father used to say about me, in the context of group sports, "Well, he's small, but he's slow." But here was something I could do relatively well—kick a football through the yellow uprights—and I did it for hours. I had a photograph on my bedroom wall of kicker Jim O'Brien following through on the field goal that won Super Bowl V for the Baltimore Colts with seconds left in the game. The camera caught him with the right kneepad of his kicking leg almost touching his face mask. The velocity of O'Brien's approach had lifted his right foot a few inches off the ground. I loved that picture. Out on the high school football field, I tried to emulate O'Brien's dynamic propulsion over and over. Though all the students were gone, the field remained oddly well maintained—grass cut low, yard lines rechalked, end zone colors sharp—as if it was waiting, hoping for the football team to return. But they never did. There was only me, kicking and retrieving, kicking and retrieving the pigskin in the imaginary game with seconds left on the clock and our team down by two.

I think perhaps my earliest pastoral impulses began on that football field, my impulse to be outdoors, alone, in bodily contact with the soil—even a manicured soil measured off at precise right angles. When I reached high school, I took up the most solitary of team sports: cross-country. It's true that there is a final team score after every meet—a combination of where the team's top five runners finished. But for 3.1 miles, you are more or less on your own, competing with yourself, your lungs, your legs. As a skinny teenager, I loved the feel of my spikes digging into the ground as we sprinted from the starting line or as I labored up a hill. I loved the long stretches on the backside of city parks when all of the runners had separated from one another, arms and hearts pumping. Wearing spikes felt intensely *animal*, like having claws. Our team mascot was the bulldog, an animal poorly bred for any kind of motion or endurance, and I secretly wanted us to be the wolverines. I wanted us to be dangerous and feral and wild. Now I'm no longer a skinny kid, and I've given up running on grass for solitary walking in woods.

Walking is the measure of thought if it's done right, if *I* do it right, if I'm not distracted by some recent misgiving or if I don't have some infuriating piece of a song buzzing around in my head on *repeat*. But if I can clear my mind and stride into the present, walking becomes an ambulatory ode to this existence. Each step affirms, over and over, that I am *here*, on the earth, in this brief moment that, when truly inhabited, might look like the fullness of time. Thus, to be alone seems to me a great act of the imagination. And of course, "to be alone with one's thoughts" is really to elect oneself to an elevated company of others. It is to choose for mental companions the past writers, artists, thinkers that mean the most to my present disposition. To commune with those predecessors in my own idiosyncratic way seems to me one of solitude's greatest gifts. Sitting in my Adirondack chair after a walk, I have the leisure to turn an idea over and over, to poke and prod it, to unspool a spider's web of jottings around it. To make it of use in my own life. To make it my own.

In his novel *A Shelter of Others*, my friend Charles Dodd White writes, "Lonely people shouldn't have to explain themselves to anybody." And I think he's right. But of course there's a difference between being lonely and being alone. Nothing seems lonelier to me than "social media," and a plethora of recent studies are linking levels of depression and even suicide to the amount of time people, especially younger people, spend staring at small screens. All of this digital company seems strangely isolating. I watch my students sit alone rather than in groups around campus, staring at their cell phones. And it isn't just my students, of course; it's everyone. If aliens came to Earth with the intent of enslaving the population, they would quickly surmise their belatedness. "These biped Earth creatures are already enslaved to a diminutive plastic god that demands their devotion at all times," the aliens would tell each other in the ethereal language of a distant galaxy. Or perhaps they would conclude that we had simply been turned into zombies, dull somnambulists whose only reality is an unreality. Because that, I think, is what these digital devices have done: robbed us of the *present*, robbed us of *presence*. We have become almost immune to our surroundings. One of the great dangers of this digital age is that it dematerializes the world—turns it into something on a screen or, worse, something to be avoided altogether. In the fall, I watch students on my campus walk past an ancient ginkgo tree whose blazing yellow leaves look like a pillar of fire, but they are oblivious; they don't see it. We can't inhabit a real place and time because, through these phones, we long to be somewhere else, with someone else. Actual experience is endlessly postponed. Existence is endlessly postponed. It becomes ever elusive because our phones promise something better is happening somewhere else. As a result, we live in what I've come to think of as the Empire of Elsewhere. It seems to me a very lonely place. Envy seems to me a very lonely emotion.

We Americans, for the most part, have never been good at being alone. Thoreau felt compelled to write an entire book to explain why he *chose* to live alone in the woods outside Concord. "Why should I feel lonely?" he wondered in the chapter of *Walden* called "Solitude"; "is not our planet in the Milky Way?" Which is to say, someone walking or watching the natural world is never really alone. In my own case, I always have the company of kingfishers, great blue herons, white-tailed deer, raccoons, yellow-rumped warblers, woodpeckers, fox squirrels, kestrels, chickadees—just to name the most constant companions. What it all adds up to, wrote Thoreau, is a "sweet and beneficent society." What it all adds up to is *health*, physical and mental. I am

at my best—my most alert, attentive, and patient—after
an hour's walk along the creek. Why? Solitude, it seems to
me, prepares us for society. We become better social creatures after we have spent time in the company of our own
thoughts, our own observations, our own inner voice that
the Stoics called our *daimon*. The prophets—Moses, Jesus,
the Buddha—always brought their message of *solidarity*
back from the wilderness, back from an intense *solitude*.
Curiously, the vision they returned with was always about
how to be more authentically social, how to be a better
people (not just a person). But that social vision had to be
born in solitude—on a mountain, in a desert, beneath a Bo
tree. The *vita activa*—the exemplary public life—could only
be learned in the *vita contemplativa*—the private mind set
apart. Only those comfortable in their skin can enter the
social realm with confidence instead of cravenness. Alone
under the Bo tree, Siddhartha realized that life's suffering
(*dukkha*) comes from futile individual craving for the *falsely*
social: fame, wealth, adulation. To find relief from that ego-
driven thirst, he said one must embark on a new path defined by compassion for others, actions and speech that do
no harm and encourage peace, an awareness of suffering
and a determination to lessen it, the mindfulness to understand the impermanence of everything, and equanimity. In
Buddhism, as I understand it, losing and finding one's self
are the same thing. The self is something that transcends
subject and object. One is simultaneously transcending the
idea of a fixed, static self and discovering a larger unfixed
self that includes all things, all beings. And both happen
best in silence, in solitude.

I think a lot about these things while I'm sitting beside Clear Creek. I hope that when I walk back up to the house, when I climb in my truck and drive to town for my teaching job, I will be more present, more empathetic, more understanding. And I hope that one thing I might teach my students, or at least help them learn, is how to be alone.

Still, perhaps the greatest and most rewarding solitary achievement is to be alone with someone else. Good friends can do this—enjoy each other's company without feeling the need to speak, to fill silence. I think a good marriage aspires to this as well. The Kentucky painter-memoirist-homesteader Harlan Hubbard spent many years living alone in a house he built on the banks of the Ohio River, across from Cincinnati. He would row his johnboat over to the Queen City to visit its public library. He became friendly with a librarian there, who seemed amused and enthralled by Hubbard's self-reliant life. One day, Hubbard slipped the woman, Anna, a note. The note proposed marriage. Hubbard would be on a certain city bus the next day at five o'clock. If Anna stepped onto the bus when it stopped at the library after work, Hubbard would take her presence there as a yes. If she didn't board the bus, he would understand. The next day at five, Anna climbed onto the bus, and the two became husband and wife, living for the next three decades on a shantyboat they floated down the Mississippi, and then at the homestead Hubbard called Payne Hollow. They raised their own food, cut their own wood for heat, and entertained themselves in the evenings with Anna on piano and Harlan on violin. After the music, they sat by the fire, sharing what Hubbard called in a wonderful phrase "a communicative silence." Like Harlan and Anna, Melissa and I have no children. And so reading late in bed on weekend mornings or sitting on the deck in the evenings, we often share this same silence that is also filled with unspoken affection. It's a symbiotic solitude that Thoreau himself longed for—he had loved a young woman from Scituate named Ellen Sewall and had probably been in love with Emerson's wife, Lidian—but never found. Hubbard and I fared better, and our lives and our solitude became much richer for it.

FREEDOM FOR THE individual, justice for the community.

BECAUSE THERE ISN'T enough sun on the bench above our house for a large garden, Melissa and I subscribe each year to a community supported agriculture project (CSA) put on by my employer, the University of Kentucky. Students in the sustainable agriculture degree program operate the CSA on the outskirts of Lexington as part of their curriculum. Their training ground is called South Farm, a tidy mix of orchards, a vineyard, and vegetable plots. Powered in large part by a solar array, South Farm is a beautiful holdout that sits at the urban intersection of a Lowes, a Walmart, and a McDonald's. The poet Richard Hugo once wrote that a city needs a river to forgive it. I would add that suburban sprawl needs a farm like this one. The Carhartt-clad students seem relentlessly cheerful and understandably proud of what they've accomplished here. If they were (or possibly, hopefully are) the future of American farming, our food system would be in excellent hands.

Most CSAs across the world work the same way: subscribers like us make a lump-sum, up-front payment in exchange for twenty-two weeks of vegetables. On Thursday afternoons from the end of May to the end of October, seventy subscribers arrive at the farm to load up our bushel baskets with a diverse assortment of organic offerings. If there's a late freeze or a disease infestation on a particular crop, well, that's the *community* part. We've all taken a chance on these young farmers, on the weather, on the increasingly hostile world that growers now face. We are *sharing* the risks as eaters. The variety of their plantings ensures that if one crop fails, another will succeed. And if you get too much of something you really don't love, like zucchini, well, that's what neighbors are for. Imagine a thousand acres of chemically treated, oil-intensive corn raised on a midwestern monoculture, and South Farm is the opposite of that.

Once, I heard an urban journalist interviewing the food writer Michael Pollan at a colloquium about CSAs. The journalist complained that when he tried subscribing to one, "the food just piled up in the refrigerator." "Well," Pollan replied, to the audience's delight, "you have to cook it." Which is to say, you have to be more deliberate about your eating. We've already paid for the vegetables and don't want them going to waste, so Melissa and I scour recipes for how we can best prepare our meals to make use of everything in our weekly haul. Such planning encourages healthier eating; we're no longer grabbing cheeseburgers on the way home from work. And food this fresh is more nutritionally dense that what we would buy in a supermarket. It also tastes a lot better than vegetables treated with ripening agents so they can sit on the shelves longer. What's more, seasonal eating from a CSA nudges one to be a more adventurous gastronomer. When Melissa pulled the purple kohlrabi, with alien-like antennae jutting from its core, she groaned, "I'm not eating that." The challenge became finding a way to prepare it so she would. I peeled off the antlers and thick skin, then cut the white flesh into matchsticks. I did the same with an apple, tossed them together with olive oil, lemon juice, salt, and pepper. It was a phenomenal little side. Melissa allowed as much. And we never would have eaten it otherwise.

When you belong to a CSA, you're supporting local farmers and farm practices that are good for the land, good for you, good for the farmer who won't be exposed to carcinogenic chemicals or mountains of debt. You are also cutting a vast number of miles off the supply chain that brought your food from farm to plate, thus reducing the amount of fossil fuels that went into the delivery of your dinner. Still, what I like best about this kind of diet is the way it reconnects me to the place where I live and the people who farm that place. I see and speak with the young farmers every week. I admire the care they take with their crops and the way they have built their soil into such a dark, hospitable loam. Our vegetables didn't come from some nameless place, some generic grocery. They came from *this* place, this soil, this careful husbandry.

I WAKE EARLY on a July morning to watch the day's first light slowly spread behind the bare silhouette branches of our walnut trees. This is my favorite kind of light: diffuse, subtle, a barely palpable blue born from gray. I love to watch this slow diffusion of color emanate above the neighboring farms and the house of a local watercolor painter. But even the most skilled watercolorist could not capture this particular shade of blue, this particular kind of light. I walk over to the window and gaze up over the trees. Venus looks like a white nail on a blue wall, a place where the passing moon will hang the coming day.

When it's all said and done, July is my favorite month in the Inner Bluegrass. When I look out the window, two Carolina wren fledglings have left the box I built for them and are perched, side by side, on the arm of my Adirondack chair. The cantaloupes trucking in from Casey County, Kentucky, are incredible. As are the tomato-and-basil-on-white-bread sandwiches I make from our garden. The Kentucky River has dropped from the ripping brown rush of spring into a quiet green slack water, perfect for my small outboard. Clear Creek is low enough that we meet many of our neighbors down by Nuptial Rock (they call it Picnic Rock, not having married there themselves). We circle up our folding chairs in a few inches of water above the riffle to catch up, splash around, swill champagne and beer. The temperature is usually perfect, there isn't much rain, and the garden is in its full glory. I move around it, weeding and tending the tomatoes, peppers, cucumbers, native pole beans. I love the smell on my fingers after pinching suckers from the tomato plants. Someone once said that the poet and novelist Thomas Hardy always smelled vaguely of the earth. *That* is a condition to which I aspire exactly.

To TURN EACH day into a work of art—what would that look like?

"THE LANDSCAPE THINKS itself in me and I am its consciousness," said the painter Paul Cézanne. It makes sense to me to think of mind, of consciousness, as an evolutionary manifestation and reflection of the world's organizing principles. Nothing could be more important to evolution's internal logic than that we feel at home here, that we feel we belong. But to feel we belong is not the same thing as to feel we were *intended*. Life, like art, comes as much from chance as from what came before—be that aesthetic or genetic design. The creative imagination thrives on chance and accidents in the same way evolution thrives on random mutations. That makes neither any less impressive. (Of the creative process, poet Charles Simic once wrote, "It's like saying, 'I wanted to go to church but the poem took me to the dog races.'") The Taoists and Buddhists of ancient China believed that human consciousness participates in the same generative—we might even say *imaginative*—process that brought the cosmos into being. Galaxies and species emerge in the world the same way images and ideas spring up in the mind. Thoughts appear and mutate like living things. The great poem, then, would come from the consciousness that feels itself an organic continuation of what *Ch'an* followers call the universe's "original mind." Cosmology and ontology would commingle like two facing mirrors. To exist in this mental space would mean to step into a timeless present that is the same present as the moment the universe thought itself into being. To exist wholly in that moment would be to suspend linear time and therefore to call the eternal into one's own consciousness. The Stoics believed something similar. They thought we all carry within us a "divine spark" that emanates from the original fire of the Creator-Creation. To feel so profoundly that stamp of the *imago dei* is to feel that consciousness is a microcosmic emanation of the macrocosm itself. Or as Ralph Waldo Emerson put it, "Ineffable is the union of man and God in every act of the soul." For Emerson, the soul is that psychic space where the human and the divine come together in a masterful overlay of the macro and the micro.

On a biological level, this is true. We still carry within us the very first, microbial forms of life. The descendants of the oxygen-breathing bacteria that emerged in primeval seas three billion years ago now exist in our own bodies as mitochondria. As the great evolutionary biologist Lynn Margulis has pointed out, we never "climbed" an evolutionary ladder out of some bacterial swamp. That bacteria colonized *us* as a suitable place to dwell—a microbiome. Thus, our bodies are a kind of history book of life on Earth. Our cells maintain a carbon- and hydrogen-rich ecosystem within our bodies, just like that of the earth when life began. Our bodies are the saline oceans of primordial seas. Our DNA derives from the same molecules in the earliest cells that formed at the edge of those first oceans. "In this way," wrote Margulis, "the microcosm lives on in us and we in it." There are more bacteria in our gut than stars in our own galaxy. Or put another way, Margulis points to a line by Charles Darwin himself that makes her case in similar, stunning imagery: "Every living creature must be looked at as a microcosm—a little universe, formed of a host of self-propagating organisms, inconceivably minute and as numerous as the stars in heaven." The microcosm of bacterial life formed from the same elements that gave birth to our macrocosmic universe.

I have always thought this a pleasing, poetic idea. But the more time I spend on the banks of Clear Creek, the more I begin to *feel* the truth Margulis discovered under the microscope in her University of Massachusetts lab. The creek itself flows like a bloodstream, while the white limestone bluffs that surround it seem like so many shoulder and hip bones. The rolling contour of the Inner Bluegrass inevitably suggests the curves of a human (animal) body. Margulis has called our attention back to the seventeenth-century scientist Sachs von Lewenheimb, who conceived of Oceanus Macro-Microcosmicus—a mythical figure that was at once a geographical landscape and a human one. Which is to say, Lewenheimb suggested that the human circulatory system functions in the same way that water flows from clouds, into rivers, into oceans, then back into clouds that then drift toward the sources of mountain streams. Just so, the four-chambered human heart pumps blood and oxygen through the body's arteries to every cell and back. Margulis and James Lovelock pushed this analogy further to argue that the earth actually *acts like* one gigantic, living organism, regulating its own moods and temperatures by cycling carbon, hydrogen, nitrogen, oxygen, phosphorus, and sulfur to maintain the climate's stability (at least until we industrialists came on the scene). Thus, if we zoomed down from space, we would observe a self-regulating planet consisting of self-regulating watersheds, consisting of self-regulating animals, consisting of self-organizing pockets of circulating energy—the nucleated cell. And that cell is a microcosm of the macrocosmic planet Earth and beyond. The sheer level of organization and analogy here is astonishing. For me, what it all adds up to is at once a biological and nearly mystical feeling of belonging. One could, of course, push the science into the realm of the spirit and say all of life is a microcosm of one macrocosmic creator. This notion would fit nicely into Spinoza's belief that the creator and the creation are one and the same—the one and the many. If so, then it would make sense that all of creation bore the stamp of the Original—the *imago dei*. We wear the embryonic stamp of the world to remind us that the world is "ensouled," as Thales said, and that the inscape is only a reflection of the landscape all around us. It wouldn't be much of a leap, then, to believe that some element of the divine still resides in all of us, all of life.

DOWN IN THE bottom beside the creek, a patch of jewelweed had grown eight feet high. Its orange and yellow flowers dangle from their stems like pendants, and they possess, to my mind, the most intricate, cunning form of all Kentucky's native wildflowers. From the side, jewelweed looks like a tiny windsock, open at the front and tapering down to what looks like a small, twisted pigtail at the back. Then, on closer inspection, the three petals on the face of the flower, one at the top and two at the bottom, are severed—they seem severed—from the sepal so that the flower begins to look more like a fish with gills. A red-speckled path leads insects into the flower's mouth, toward the nectary at the back of the sepal. When a hawk moth dives down into the sepal's narrow cave, it brushes the anther that hangs down from above and actually changes the flower from male to female, just like that. The stamen becomes a pistil, so when the same hawk moth enters another flower, it pollinates the hanging ovary. And it retrieves some nectar. An equitable exchange is transacted.

But why am I talking in metaphors of money, a language that debases this natural economy? Let me say instead that jewelweed has hit upon a brilliant strategy, a brilliant design for survival. But that's a sentence that also carries loaded words: *strategy* and *design*. The first suggests the jewelweed flower is the product of evolution, the second that it is the work of a just and deliberate creator. And indeed, it strikes me that if a creationist and an evolutionist examined this flower, as I am doing now, they would each reach their own presumptions and conclusions. On the one hand: "Only God could have created something so complex and beautiful." On the other: "Obviously, this flower evolved into this manifestation as the most efficient way to lure bees and distribute pollen." Of course, we could say both are right if we're willing to assume that the hand of God works *through* evolution, but that explanation will usually satisfy neither party. The evolutionist says, "Leave God out of this," and the creationist says, "Leave evolution out of God."

Still, there are many scientists and many religious people—even four popes—who are willing to split the difference in the name of *theistic evolutionism*. The only trouble with this is that to admit God works through evolution, one is also forced to admit that God's work is incredibly violent, perhaps even sadistic. After all, *Glyptapanteles* wasps inject their eggs into the bowels of caterpillars, and then the wasp larvae devour the vital organs of the caterpillar, killing it from the inside out. What benevolent or just God would think that up? Charles Darwin mulled that question over and over as he made the transition from his family's (and his wife's) religion to his own agnosticism. To believe God works through evolution would mean to abandon Christianity's understanding of a loving deity, but then again, I think that's as it should be. To anthropomorphize what we call God into some humanlike, interventionist father figure who shares our values because he bestowed them on us in the first place strikes me as an amazing failure of the imagination. It's the projection of a fearful consciousness that wants to know why we suffer and whether meaning can be found in that suffering. Out of those questions emerge all the systems of religious law and moral strictures. And out of those dogmatic absolutes grow intolerance, bigotry, and terror (perhaps the best argument that Buddhism isn't a religion is that nobody kills anyone else in its name). Better, I think, to admit we can know nothing about the sublime force of creation other than what we observe in the natural world. If you can't know the mind of this God, then you cannot tell others what to think. You cannot kill or behead someone in the name of that God. You cannot justify misogyny, homophobia, or racism. You can only stand in wonder.

As FOR THIS, the sixth great, human-induced extinction: tell the God of Job—the voice of the whirlwind—that we knew better than he.

IN THE CALENDAR created by the Jacobins of the French Revolution, the month we call July, they called Thermidor. The word comes from the Greek, meaning "summer heat." And it is hot and humid out on the island rock. Sunfish and smallmouth dart under and around it. Butterflies called commas and question marks punctuate the woods. The sound of cuckoos and thrushes are barely audible over the riffle just upstream. There's a tired, dry feel to the woods. Buckeye leaves are beginning to brown and curl at their tips. And this is the hottest July on record. In fact, the last five years have been the five hottest years on record.

A few facts: All but one of the earth's mass extinctions have been caused by climate change. According to the UN, there will be two hundred million climate refugees by 2050. The world's richest 7 percent are responsible for *half* of the world's carbon dioxide emissions. The poorest 50 percent are responsible for only 7 percent of emissions. And they are suffering the most from climate change—a tragedy of inversion. I could trot out a legion of other statistics, but the majority of Americans don't seem moved by facts and statistics. Nor do they seem moved by stories of vanishing species or exposés about the many corporations that are pumping CO_2 and methane into the atmosphere.* Why? Because too many Americans don't want to believe in anything—science or a new set of ethics—that would reign in an entire culture and an entire economy built on fossil fuels. They'll believe

---

* They don't even seem moved by the science that shows toxic synthetic chemicals like dioxin magnify as they move up the food chain until they wind up in breast milk.

instead in a religion that will lift us *out* of this world and into another. But a religion that calls on us to be stewards *here and now*—we in the United States have no use for that. Winston Churchill once said Americans always do the right thing—after we've tried every other option. I think about that quite a bit with regard to climate change. When we're choking on the fires in California, being swept away by the hurricanes down South, watching our livestock drown in the floods of the Midwest, dying of heatstroke in the Southwest, then we Americans might finally rouse ourselves into action. And by then—if *then* is in more than three decades—it will be too late.

Environmentalists have spent many frustrating decades trying to figure out how they—we—might cut through such monumental apathy and ignorance. My answer is we can't. Anti-intellectualism in this country, coupled with corporate power and political mendacity, is simply too great. The only thing that will rouse us to collective action, as Churchill understood, is the specter of catastrophe. Should we then resign ourselves to a burning world and just wait it out with the anesthetizing distractions of YouTube and Netflix? That seems too cowardly to me. I've been fighting these fights long enough to know my side loses far, far more than it wins. But what's worse than losing, it seems to me, is losing without dignity. Abdication. Acquiescence. We should instead listen to the Stoics, who said we should do the right thing *simply because* it is the right thing to do. In 1931, my fellow Kentuckian Florence Reece, the wife of a labor organizer, wrote the greatest union song of all time, "Which Side Are You On?" The title poses a simple question. It's not "Who do you think will win?" but rather "Where do you stand?" Do you stand on the side of conscience or on the side of self-interest? Again, a simple question. I put it out there.

A WOODEN BOAT is a living thing and a Buddhist lesson in impermanence. As a result, it needs near-constant attention, devotion even. Like Henry David Thoreau, I have built two wooden boats in my life. "If rightly made," Thoreau wrote, "a boat would be a sort of amphibious animal, a creature of two elements, related by one half its structure to some swift and shapely fish, and by the other to some strong-winged and graceful bird." Because Kentucky is landlocked, we have little wind along our waterways, and so my own boats are more fish than fowl. That is to say, when building them, I didn't bother trying to rig a sail I would rarely use. The first boat I built was a rowing dory called a Gloucester Gull. It's a beautiful boat with low, sweeping lines and a narrow "tombstone" transom—the kind of skiff nineteenth-century New England whalers, armed with rocket harpoons, would hoist from the deck of their schooners in pursuit of the coveted *spermaceti* lamp oil. When we moved out to Nonesuch, I decided I wanted a boat that could get up and down the river a little faster than human propulsion affords. So I built a fifteen-foot runabout that stretches five feet at the beam and is fitted with a low-emission, six-horsepower outboard (suffice to say it can't be mistaken for one of those amped-up bass boats you see careening across lakes and rivers here in the South).

To my thinking, a small wooden boat, built with carvel

planking, is the most beautiful artifact to ever rise from the human mind and take shape beneath human hands. I have whiled away many mornings with a pot of coffee, studying photos and plans for the Adirondack guide boat, the Whitehall rowing boat, the Annapolis Wherry, and many others. It never felt like a waste of time. It felt like watching a poem take on a physical form. And it made me think of all those ancient Chinese poems that were actually written in small boats, flooded with moonlight, along the Yangtze River. Now of course, in the age of mass production, the wooden boat is an anachronism. Which makes me love it all the more. In a wonderful little essay called "A Man's Leisure Time," the naturalist Aldo Leopold contemplates the satisfaction of hobbies. His is talking about his own hobby, carving wooden archery bows, but he could just as well be talking about boatbuilding: "I am tempted to conclude that a satisfactory hobby must be in large degree useless, inefficient, laborious, or irrelevant. Certainly many of our most satisfying avocations today consist of making something by hand which machines can usually make more quickly and cheaply, and sometimes better." Such a hobby, says Leopold, is a defiance of the contemporary, a solitary revolt against the commonplace. Building my boats was certainly laborious and inefficient. Your standard American boat company can produce in a couple of days what took me the better part of a year. But I would wager the man who buys such a boat feels none of the exuberant defiance of the commonplace and the contemporary as I do when I guide my boat along the rivers and lakes of Kentucky.

Somewhere, I read that, when weaving prayer rugs,

Buddhist monks intentionally include a mistake in the pattern as a lesson in humility. Well, my boat is a long sermon on the subject. Its flaws are legion, but as a whole, the *Motsie Jane* (a nickname Melissa's grandmother gave her) still takes on a satisfying form, one well-suited to the windless gorge through which the Kentucky River flows. But as I said, she needs care. This week, I removed the motor and flipped her over in the front yard to work on the hull—puttying divots, reapplying fiberglass cloth and resin, adding yet another coat of blue paint. With that done, I sanded smooth the peeling thwarts, then spread on three layers of ship varnish. When that dried, all signs of a harsh winter wrapped only in a thin tarp were behind us. Today, the *Motsie Jane* gleams again, and I hook her up to the back of my truck and head for the boat ramp.

I live in the Kentucky River watershed, and I'm launching my boat on the river today because I want to float beneath these limestone palisades and think about the political potential of that fact. I also want to head about ten miles upstream to check on a heron rookery that last year filled the crown of a sycamore tree. The only place to put in on this stretch of the river is at a ramp surrounded by a raggedy assortment of trailers, where the Confederate South is still well represented in both symbols and a vague sense of foreboding. Creedence Clearwater Revival famously sang that "people on the river are happy to give"; however, that has almost never been my experience. But in early morning, no one is stirring, and I ease my boat quietly into the water, crank the motor, and speed away.

When I get about five miles upstream, I cut the motor

and settle down in a small canvas chair placed between the thwarts. I take out a blue book and in it start to opine thusly: By definition, a watershed is simply a more or less bowl-shaped landform that, because of its highest points and because of gravity, drains into one river basin. There are eight major watersheds in Kentucky. This particular one, which provides drinking water to a sixth of the state, covers about seven thousand square miles and has a tributary network of over fifteen thousand miles. The river's three main forks come alive in the mountains of Eastern Kentucky and converge near the Red River Gorge, where the mainstream then meanders on toward its embouchure at the Ohio River, near Cincinnati. That's the geography of my watershed, but as I said, I want to think about the politics, because while states and nations draw artificial geographical boundaries, watersheds draw real ones. For that reason alone, I would prefer—and propose to anyone who might listen—a radically decentralized system of governance in this country that is based on the actual borders mapped by every watershed. The eight watersheds of Kentucky would become eight nearly autonomous cantons (to use the Swiss term and analogy). But I actually have one other reason for thinking about such a proposal. It seems an inviolable rule that the larger a country grows, the more corrupt it becomes, and right now, we Americans are living in an almost irredeemably corrupt country. Powerful corporations have used their money to buy off politicians, who use their influence to further enrich the already rich and, in the service of their corporate masters, weaken all manner of regulations put in place to protect the general public from physical and financial harm. Other large per capita countries like China, Russia, and India reinforce this general theory of corruption, albeit through other avenues of influence, while small countries like Norway, Denmark, Switzerland, and Japan offer models of citizen well-being, environmental health, and political transparency. But in a country as large as the US, wealth and power inevitably become centralized in the hands of the few. One percent of Americans control 80 percent of the country's total wealth, and as a result, the United States remains a republic in name only. That concentration of wealth, along with the absurd idea that one member of Congress could adequately represent 700,000 constituents, has made Americans feel politically powerless. And the result of that powerlessness has taken three forms: a withdrawal from political participation, a deep distrust of the federal government, and a tendency to blame problems on minorities and immigrants. The moneyed and corporate elite, along with the old white men they bankroll in Congress, encourage all three of these responses because a disillusioned electorate makes their kleptocratic schemes all the easier to deploy, and the focus on "free-riding" minorities distracts much of the public from Congress members' real task—further enriching the already rich. For instance, scientists from the Environmental Protection Agency have proven that Dow Chemical's pesticide, chlorpyrifos, causes brain damage in children at even low levels of exposure. And yet the industry-approved head of that very agency (under the Trump administration), tasked with protecting the nation's health, refused to ban it. And there are thousands of examples just like this one that all point to the same conclusion: the concentration of power and wealth in a country so large that its citizens can be completely ignored has led to a state of degeneracy that is quickly bringing the American experiment to an end.

Given all that, why not try a new experiment that would be the exact opposite of a bloated, venal federal government? There are 482 major watersheds in the lower forty-eight states. Each is geographically "sovereign" in the sense that by its physical boundaries, a watershed is self-sufficient. It circulates its own natural wealth over and over. It generates no waste and does not "externalize" (as economists say) the "cost of production" onto other rivers and valleys. In a watershed, all energy (sun, wind, and water) is renewable, and all resource use is dynamically balanced and sustainable. One river basin doesn't borrow or steal energy or resources from other watersheds. Compare a healthy watershed to the most unnatural of landscapes, a strip mine, which causes erosion and flooding, despoils air and water, and contributes drastically to our climate crisis. A watershed, by contrast, purifies air and water, holds soil in place while enriching it, and sequesters carbon. Thus, not only is a watershed self-sufficient, it is conservative, symbiotic, decentralized, and diverse. A healthy watershed conserves its water and stores its sunlight. The more species a watershed supports, the more likely they all will thrive and the less likely an exotic insect will decimate any one species.

What I'm now suggesting is that we apply those natural principles to politics. Why not return to the spirit of this country's original Articles of Confederation and make each watershed its own sovereign province? One could easily argue, after all, that Alexander Hamilton, James Madison, and their well-to-do, mostly slave-owning friends who met in Philadelphia for the Constitutional Convention were determined to move democratic power away from the common, mostly agrarian people and into the hands of wealthier Americans. When soldiers from George Washington's Continental Army were thrown in debtors' prisons because they hadn't been paid for their military service and thus couldn't pay their taxes, Daniel Shays led a pitchfork-wielding band of farmers through the streets of Springfield, Massachusetts, heading toward the courthouse and the federal arsenal, looking for restitution. That rebellion spooked the "founding fathers" enough to quickly draw up a constitution that would take wealth and power away from the states. What's more, anti-federalists like George Mason argued no national government would "suit so extensive a country, embracing so many climates, and containing inhabitants so very different in manners, habits, and customs." Under a federal constitution, argued Madison, the role of government would be to "protect the minority of the opulent against the majority." And our increasingly centralized federal government has been doing that ever since.

Why not return to the Western world's original democracy, the Athenian *polis*, where communal decisions were made by a popular assembly, the *ecclesia*? I'm not advocating for the abolition of the federal government. There would still remain the need for a (vastly smaller) military to protect the confederation of watersheds. We would need uniform civil rights and environmental protections, immigration and asylum guidelines, along with a federal strategy to fight pandemics, natural disasters, and climate change. As for the now hopelessly outdated Constitution, I would argue, along with Harvard-educated lawyer Elie Mystal, that we should hold on to the First and Fourteenth Amendments of the Bill of Rights. Everything else could be relegated down to the watershed cantons. Let them write their own constitutions. For the last five decades, we've heard self-serving calls from the right for smaller government, and thus less regulation of Wall Street and environmental atrocities. As someone who politically identifies with the democratic-socialist philosophy of my Scandinavian ancestors, I'm not for a bigger role for government. I'm for a much smaller role for corporate capitalists. In his essay "Civil Disobedience," Thoreau famously wrote that he wanted smaller government as well but added this crucial caveat—"when men are prepared for it." It is quite easy to look around this country and see that we are in no way prepared for it. There is simply no way to talk about "shrinking government" while standing in the shadows of corporate predation. The only way to shrink government is to simultaneously shrink the power of those corporations. But as of now, as soon as the federal government decides it should not regulate corporations or banks, the coal industry will flood mountain streams with toxic metals, the pharmaceutical industry will flood the streets with opioids, the chemical industry will flood farms with cancerous pesticides, and the financial industry will flood the market with debt and toxic securities. The Right's constant call for freedom *from* governmental constraint is really a demand for the freedom *to* abuse the public—financially, environmentally, and physically in terms of health. My point being, the economic system known as capitalism could only function benignly on a strictly local level, where consumers know producers and where communities can protect themselves from corporate charlatans. But capitalism as practiced on the national and international level has shown itself to be a human and ecological disaster. It tears from the earth 25 percent more resources than can be sustainably replaced. The profits from all that extraction are funneled up to the wealthy plutocrats, and the toxic by-products are externalized—dumped—onto poor countries and poor communities. Then the United States takes one-fourth of every tax dollar to finance a military that ensures continual, uncontested access to the rest of the world's natural resources. We have eight hundred military bases in eighty countries, yet we can't keep lead out of the drinking water in Flint, Michigan, or selenium out of it in the mountains of Appalachia. In 2020, we couldn't make enough ventilators to save hundreds of thousands of lives.

My teacher, the writer Guy Davenport, once wrote, "Distance negates responsibility." And it's true on both ends: distance from the people being exploited allows the powerful not to think too much about them, and the same distance makes the powerless feel they have no recourse to hold the powerful to account. But a watershed confederacy might change all that. It would return responsibility back to the level of the local. Federal taxes would be greatly diminished because, for one thing, small, self-sufficient regions wouldn't need to wage international wars over resources and trade. There would be no federal taxes for education, health care, agriculture, housing, or welfare because decisions and responsibility for all of those would revert to each individual watershed. Local governments and *ecclesias*—better known in this country as community town halls—would decide all matters related to education, health care, policing, gun control, public assistance, the regulation of corporations, and incarceration. And each watershed would decide how it wants to raise revenue for schools, community improvement projects, and social services. Faced with the responsibility of self-governance, Americans would have to relearn the art of citizenship. The Angry White Working Class that now so resents the federal government would have nowhere to place, or displace, its resentment, except on itself.

A watershed economy is by definition a local economy. As in Thomas Jefferson's dream for this country, it produces as much as it can within the watershed before looking to import goods from other places. Perhaps it even has its own currency that can keep local wealth circulating longer within that community instead of leaving it. After all, the more self-sufficient and diverse a community, the more resilient it becomes against predatory corporations—invasive species—that feel no responsibility to its people or its landscapes. What's more, by producing as much as it can locally, a watershed community cuts the length of supply lines, lessening both its dependence on fossil fuels and its contribution to climate change.

A watershed economy asks, What are this region's greatest assets and what can it produce with the least harm to the land and the people? It doesn't, for instance, drain its water table dry to grow almonds for export. Nor does it produce energy through means that would harm other

watersheds—through the burning of coal that acceler-
ates climate change everywhere and pollutes air and water
downstream, beyond its borders. Rather, a watershed ethos
asks how the watershed can best harness the renewable
energy within its own ecosystem. Beyond that, consider
what a region would look like if it socialized all of the services—water, electricity, lending, sanitation, infrastructure
building, health care—where right now a private corporation usually stands to benefit at the public's expense. In my
own ideal version of the watershed canton, all such services
would be operated by worker-owned cooperatives. Freed
from the profit motive, such co-ops would have far better
environmental records, and all of their wealth would be returned to the men and women who actually created them,
who actually provided the services. Additional profits raised
from water and electric bills would be put into a trust, out
of which every citizen in the watershed would be paid an
annual dividend, just as Alaskans receive now for their oil.

The watershed economy would also divorce economic activity from environmental damage. It would ask its members what they want to consume and what they want to
produce. The decision would be theirs and not the whim
of some great advertising machine or extractive industry.
It would emphasize work based on useful services rather
than on wasteful, resource-intensive "growth." That is to
say, it would emphasize work that cannot be outsourced and
that adds quality to the community. The nineteenth-century
British artist-writer-socialist William Morris said we should
not own anything that isn't either beautiful or useful. The
same applies to work: we should concentrate on jobs that

add beauty and use to our communities. I'm thinking of teachers, health-care workers, carpenters, mechanics, landscapers, plumbers, coaches, architects, engineers, jewelry makers, store owners, organic farmers, therapists, restaurateurs who serve locally grown food, musicians and artists, construction workers, local bankers, and many other such *value-added* occupations. I'm *not* thinking of telemarketers, insurance salesmen, lobbyists, actuaries, PR flacks, advertisers. A recent survey found that about 30 percent of Americans think their jobs are useless, unsatisfying, or both. Such jobs should either be eliminated or automated. I'm thinking about an economy based on pleasure, need, and purpose, not accumulation and toxic waste. Monetary capital and social capital both would flow throughout the watershed, building wealth, trust, and good feeling through every exchange. Citizens would no longer be at the mercy of far-off banks they have to bail out through no fault of their own.

Rather, each watershed's lending agencies might closely resemble the Bank of North Dakota, which was created one hundred years ago when a populist movement swept across the northern plains. Farmers, angry that eastern banks and markets determined who got loans and how goods were marketed, took over the state legislature and created their own bank, which became the depository for all state revenue. Today, those deposits are plowed back into the state through very low-interest loans to farmers, students, local businesses, and other economic development projects. The Bank of North Dakota made the first federally insured student loan, in 1967. It doesn't engage in dubious speculative

behavior like subprime lending, derivatives, or credit default
swaps. As a result, during the financial collapse of 2008 the
Bank of North Dakota and the state as a whole inoculated
themselves against such centralized failures. Beyond all that,
in an average year, the bank pays something like a $60 mil-
lion dividend back to the state's general fund. Contrast all
of that to your average private commercial bank. Through
a process called fractional reserve lending, a bank can loan
out thirty times the money it actually has on reserve. Thus,
banks literally loan into existence money they don't have,
then charge interest on that money—interest they did nothing to earn. To pay back that interest, the borrower has to
find money that didn't exist before, forcing the economy to
constantly expand at the expense of the borrower and the
natural world. If a bank loans out $100 at 5 percent inter-
est, that $5 has to be dug out of the ground somewhere. In
fact, by the time we buy, say, a new computer, half of its cost
will be comprised of interest charged at every stage of production. All of that interest will accrue in the hands of the
wealthy bankers, and all of the debt will take the form of
the need for ever-expanding, unsustainable economic activity, or "growth." Perhaps it's worth mentioning here that the
world's three dominant monotheistic religions all condemn
such usury in their scriptures because lenders, who did not
labor for the money, take it from those who did.

The currency system in this country exists primarily to benefit the already rich. In 1913, J. P. Morgan convinced Woodrow Wilson to push through the Federal
Reserve Act three days before Christmas, when members
of Congress were otherwise preoccupied. Thus, the Federal

Reserve—which is neither federal nor a reserve—allowed a private central bank to print its own money and exchange it for government bonds. That bank could then create money out of nothing and lend it to the government at interest. What sane government would have ever agreed to taking on that level of debt for no other reason than to enrich private commercial banks? At the time, senator Charles Lindbergh Sr. fumed, "The financial system has been turned over to a purely profiteering group. The system is private, conducted for the sole purpose of obtaining the greatest possible profits from the use of other people's money." Just consider what would happen if the Federal Reserve actually *was* part of the federal government: the money it generates would go into the US Treasury, erasing federal debt to fund bonds and potentially making Americans' taxes much lower. As Ellen Hodgson Brown writes in her eye-peeling study *The Web of Debt*, the federal income tax was created in the same year as the Federal Reserve "primarily to secure a reliable source of money to pay the interest due to the bankers on the government's securities." Her solution—a damn good one it seems to me—is to bypass the banks and let the federal government create its own money, just as Abraham Lincoln did to fund the Northern campaign during the Civil War. That would eliminate the need for an income tax, and personal taxes could be lowered further if we shifted them from productive activity, like work and income, to unproductive activity, like short-selling stocks and pumping carbon into the atmosphere (a 0.0003 percent tax on Wall Street trading, incidentally, would raise $35 billion a year). I would take Brown's ideas a step further and say, in the same spirit that created the Bank of North Dakota, let each watershed issue its own currency (as the Constitution allows) through its own bank, a people's bank. That would take usurious lenders out of the equation, and it would also create a currency that couldn't be used as a commodity, that would indeed be worthless to Wall Street. The community bank would follow the traditional banker's motto of 3-6-3: pay 3 percent interest on savings, charge 6 percent interest on loans, and be at the golf course by 3:00 p.m. All of the money that the bank makes through interest payments would be put back into the community—into its schools, infrastructure needs, pensions, and social services. All projects proposed to improve social life in the watershed would be funded by no-interest loans, just as Denmark and Sweden have been doing for decades. College students would also be given interest-free loans, or better yet, the interest accumulated through the watershed bank might pay for all students' tuition. The obscene profits of bankers would be replaced by lower taxes and funding for all of these social investments.

A confederacy of self-sufficient, decentralized watersheds would also go a long way toward alleviating the great gap in this country between what we now refer to as red and blue states. Each faction would spend far less time hating individual presidents and members of Congress simply because those elected officials would no longer wield that much power over the lives of Americans. What's more, those same Americans would be busy doing the real work of self-governance, which in turn would give them a sense of self-determinacy and empowerment that seems lost now and seems to fuel so much partisan anger. We would find ourselves thrown into closer contact with the people we demonize online, and that contact would inevitably force us to reexamine the caricatures we have created of one another. The labels of blue and red, conservative and liberal, would reveal themselves as pointless procrustean beds in the face of the real, messy work of making decisions about what's best for one's watershed. Here in Kentucky, one finds a great deal of suspicion and resentment of liberal states like California, Massachusetts, and New York—the very states that pay a vastly disproportionate amount of tax dollars that go to help the poor, the unemployed, and the disabled people of this state. But all of that federal welfare, all of that redistribution, has done little good for the Big Sandy River Basin of Eastern Kentucky, which remains the poorest and sickest place in the country.

Perhaps it's time for the Big Sandy watershed to take responsibility for itself and for its Angry White Working Class to stop blaming outsiders for its problems. After all, the real outsiders who wrecked the region aren't California and New York liberals but coal operators from St. Louis, Ohio, and Florida. In "Black Waters," a ballad I know by heart, Jean Ritchie sings about the strip miners, "If I had ten million, somewheres thereabout, / Well, I'd buy Perry County and throw them all out." Well, that would have been a good start. But the reality is the strip miners will soon be leaving anyway. All of the profitable seams of coal have now been mined out, the water is nearly undrinkable, and the country is turning toward other energy sources. My contention is that building an economy and a system of self-governance around the common experience of sharing a watershed could be unifying and inspiring. A watershed democracy encourages *real* pride in a place, not the empty patriotism that is so often on display is this bloated country.

I'll return once more to my model of a forest, because there is one in Eastern Kentucky that I know quite well. I've taken my students there for many years, and I've spent a decent amount of time and words trying to keep strip miners and loggers out of it. It's called Robinson Forest, and it spans fifteen thousand contiguous acres. The forest is owned by my employer, the University of Kentucky, and unfortunately, UK trustee members, along with state legislators, have spent decades trying to turn its natural resources into millions of coal dollars. But recently, UK entered into a partnership with the Nature Conservancy's Working Woodlands program, which certifies that trees will remain standing as capturers of carbon. It then sells those carbon credits as offsets to airlines and other companies or individuals. Estimates show there's about $5 million worth of carbon captured by the trees of Robinson Forest.

It's obviously time for the citizens of the Big Sandy watershed to get together and think about what will make the region flourish in the post-coal era. Robinson Forest shows that could include an economy built around carbon markets, reforestation, sustainable timbering, and renewable energy. The forest shows it should also include capturing sunlight in the form of sprawling arrays of now-affordable solar panels stretched out across the southern faces of old strip mines. The pot plants that now grow illicitly in the forest (I've often stumbled upon them) even show that legalizing marijuana could greatly improve the economy and simultaneously do something to alleviate the region's opioid epidemic. The watershed needs health-care workers; Melissa argues that it would be an ideal, affordable place for retirement communities. The natural world, after all, is a healing place, and there is still a great deal of natural beauty in Eastern Kentucky. It's time now for the watershed to finally take a lesson from its forests. What looks now like one of the poorest places in the country, thanks to an extractive industry that gave nothing back, is actually a place of great natural wealth, wealth that could be tapped by local people working together for their own common good.

The American philosopher Richard Rorty has written succinctly that the real point of any government should be to reduce suffering and increase sympathy. I would add that the point of a watershed economy is to decrease corruption and increase justice. I realize, of course, that what I've just proposed sounds "utopian," hence "naive," "unrealistic," "irrelevant." But consider the pandemic that just swept across the globe. Disease is largely the product of cities and civilizations because cities crowd out wildlife and encourage people to crowd together in unhealthy and disproportionate ways. Evolutionary biologists deploy a useful term: *density dependent population regulation.* It basically means that when places move beyond their carrying capacity, competition, parasitism, and disease are the results. Surely that's what was and is happening with COVID-19. Nature is sending us a message. It is culling the herd—and the herd is us. If we don't voluntarily resettle in the Jeffersonian cantons I've just described, future pandemics and climate change might eventually force us into them anyway, though in a much more chaotic and violent fashion. Concentrated cities will very likely become too disease-ridden, too violent, and too hot, given all that reflective glass and asphalt. We might be forced back—but perhaps, also forward—into the kind of smaller human bands that were our genetic and geographic home for almost all of our evolutionary past. Such a social reconfiguration might be brutal and violent . . . or it might not. Consider the ways humans almost always react to natural disasters like Katrina, the San Francisco earthquake, or the tornado that destroyed Mayfield, Kentucky, in 2021. The initial reports out of New Orleans of roving gangs, killings, and rapes were almost all wrong. In reality, hundreds of people brought boats and supplies to help those stranded by floodwaters. The Disaster Research Center at the University of Delaware concluded that the overwhelming response was "prosocial in nature." The center also has shown that in nearly seven hundred disasters since 1963, the majority of people almost always responded with calm and compassion. In situations where the government apparatus of law and order suddenly disappears, our "lawless" better angels emerge.

To live inside the hierarchical political construct called the *state* is actually quite unnatural, though four hundred years after the invention of cities, we have a hard time seeing it as such. The first states only came into being about six thousand years ago, and even back four hundred years, one-third of the planet was populated by hunters, gatherers, and pastoralists. We never *naturally* chose to live within a state. Why would someone give up the freedom, the leisure, and the excitement of hunting, for example, to adopt the drudgery and routine of dawn-to-dusk farm-ing? (What's more, it was those Paleolithic hunting cultures that have some of the greatest—and earliest—art, painted on cave walls in Australia, Indonesia, France, and Spain.) There's a reason the founding fathers of this country en-slaved Africans to do that work; they violated every moral law known to man to avoid such labor. No, the political state was *forced* upon us, and we were coerced into inhab-iting it. The state, as anthropologist James C. Scott has shown in his excellent book *Against the Grain*, was obsessed with two things: controlling the reproduction of grain, an-imals, women, and slaves, and collecting taxes. No one other than a powerful, wealthy minority of men would have chosen any of those oppressive measures. Thus, on some level, we have been trying to escape those brutal state sys-tems since the French Revolution, with mixed and minimal results. But still, I would argue there is a progressive, eman-cipatory form of politics that runs from French republican-ism to Scandinavian democratic socialism to a more radical form of socialism based on worker-owned cooperatives and finally to the ultimate manifestation of liberty—political anarchism. I'm not talking about the juvenile, fuck-you an-archism of a punk band like the Sex Pistols (whose motto was "cash for chaos"); I'm talking about a school of po-litical thought founded by William Godwin, Pierre-Joseph Proudhon, Mikhail Bakunin, and Emma Goldman. As the American anarchist Edward Abbey once wrote, "Anarchism doesn't mean no rules, it means no rulers." The political definition of anarchism is quite simple: All forms of human organization ought to be voluntary. Free communities are bound together by common economic and social interests and are arranged by mutual agreement. There can be no institutional power except the power of people cooperating under free contract. As political theorist Crispin Sartwell writes, "Anyone who holds that legitimate state power can only rest on the consent of the governed is an anarchist." Today, we are born into oppressive political systems not of our choosing, and Black men in the US are essentially born into a police state. Anarchism simply renounces all institutions that curtail our freedom without our consent. Thus, the watershed economy I'm envisioning is a form of socialist-anarchism that is the opposite of chaos and disorder. It would not mean irresponsibility but rather radical acts of responsibility whereby a people truly govern themselves.

Well, all of these ravings have now filled two blue books in the two hours I've been moored here. For much of that time, a damselfly, with its delicate emerald body and black wings, watched from the corner of my clipboard while my boat slowly spun in a slight breeze. But now the buzzards are circling a little lower, getting a little more brazen, a little more curious. So I hoist anchor and head upriver until I see the many ministrations of an active great blue heron colony. In the crown of a large, riverside sycamore, these adult *herodians* have built their rookery of a dozen nests, all about three feet across and loosely assembled with sticks and soft grasses. If I had arrived earlier in the year, I might have witnessed the herons' inspired courtship rituals. High in the tree, a male and female pair will sway in unison, with their long bills pointed skyward and clacking together. The male, with his handsome, slicked-back crest, will then commence a circular nuptial flight above his perched, prospective mate. Finally, he'll retrieve sticks for the family nest, just to prove he's up to any filial tasks. Today, the fledglings are already hatched and hungry, and the parents are busy foraging for fish and salamanders. Often, the blue heron will spear a small fish and then flip it headfirst down the gullet. Some gluttons have even been known to choke on oversized prey. But herons always look graceful in flight as they fold their long necks into a tight S and glide above the river. The noisiness of this heronry will keep most predators away, but if a raccoon does try to climb up in search of a small meal, the immature heron will defend itself by emptying its bowels over the side of the nest in a foul-smelling shower that usually sends the stymied hunter scurrying back to the river. But if he waits patiently below, the raccoon can usually count on some fledglings being pushed accidentally out of the crowded nests. First-year mortality in many heronries can climb as high as 70 percent. But today, all of the young seem accounted for, though the sycamore itself appears to be finally dying from years of intensive guano droppings around its base. Once on Clear Creek, I startled a heron in mid-defecation. It abruptly took flight and left a long, white calligraphy shimmering on the surface of the water. Thus, given their scatological excess, I watch the herons hunt and gather from a safe distance. And for a moment, it strikes me that this rookery might have found a counterpart in the nineteenth century, when a band of Shakers built their own tight, industrious community on the headlands high above this river. Like the sycamore, that community died out too. But not because the Shaker vision proved unworkable. The Kentucky Shakers were doomed by the industrial ugliness that followed the Civil War and that I can glimpse right now in the form of two smokestacks belching carcinogens at the E. W. Brown Generating Station. The plant was built on the Dix River to harness hydroelectric power, but its administrators soon found it cheaper to buy strip-mined coal from the TVA, which had itself abandoned clean hydropower for the infernal destructiveness of coal. The mountains of Eastern Kentucky were leveled to power plants like this one, and the Shakers' vision of a heaven on earth succumbed to the industrial dream of a world consuming itself with the fire next time—the fire that is now burning across the globe. Even here, surrounded by beautiful limestone palisades and regal blue herons, I can't escape it. I can only take pleasure in this short reprieve and in my own solitary scribblings about a world we might actually want.

THERE ARE TWO moralities: one based on fear and one based on conscience. The first is the morality of the state, of the church, of the penal system. The second is the morality of the individual, the cooperative. A god that is not a lawgiver but a shape-shifter takes up new forms in every living thing, in every soul. This kind of god makes life richer, more varied, not narrower and flat. A lawgiving god is a distant god. A shape-shifting god exists inside every tissue of our being. Another way of saying this: Morality locks us into a past; imagination frees us into the present and makes a future possible.

THERE IS A swimming hole along Clear Creek that is, as far as I'm concerned, the best-kept secret in Central Kentucky. It's hard to reach, so few make the effort. But the effort is well worth the arrival. Melissa and I, along with our painter friend, Johnny Lackey, and his wife, Jenny, park my truck at the end of our lane, at a place the neighbors call the Point. It's a high headland that hangs about fifty feet above the creek. We grab our cooler, strap tractor-tire inner tubes across our torsos, then head off across the gray limestone esplanade that's lined with wind-twisted cedars and prickly pear cactus, the only cactus native to Kentucky. From the edge of the bluff, we watch a pair of belted kingfishers darting through the trees below us, and it strikes me that this is the only time I've actually seen the *back* of this bird—it's blue-gray plumage and white wing bars. Soon, we're descending through a narrow cleft in the rock that functions something like an asymmetrical, Marcel Duchamp staircase. We grasp at cedar limbs for balance, search for solid footfall. Just when it looks like we can go no further, another passageway presents itself, and we climb on down. Finally, we emerge through chinquapins and imbricated rock at a shelf that marks the mouth of a dry creek bed. Just below it is a stone-enclosed pool, and beyond that, framed by two pretty riffles, a perfect stretch of still water—the best-kept secret.

We park our cooler on the spit that divides the pool and the swimming hole. Male sunfish are busy attending two nests there in the shallows. I watch a three-foot longnose gar shimmy past. Then, beers in hand, we fall back into our tubes and let the momentum carry us out into the middle

of the creek. We drift beneath the indomitable gray fortress we just navigated around. Tough little ferns have taken root in thin humus that has accumulated in the cliff's small pittings. Whites and skippers, the most ephemeral of all life, flutter against this obdurate wall of limestone, where every ripple on the surface of the water is reflected in shimmering waves. In less than half an hour, we have descended millions of years from high bank to creek bed. I stare from that past, up to the yellow cacti that hangs over the rim rock, and it occurs to me that we are floating, however fleetingly, along the bottom of time.

"I loaf and invite my soul," Walt Whitman famously writes to begin "Song of Myself." We do the same, drifting here on a hot summer day with no other souls in sight. Johnny, an excellent landscape painter and wood engraver, takes a small camera from a ziplock bag and starts clicking away for future source material. Once, I traded Johnny a wooden coffee table I had built for a hand-colored wood engraving of a landscape that looks much like this. I think I got the better part of that deal, and the piece hangs in our kitchen against the wall fashioned from the stones that once made up the dam at Ford's Mill.

As we float, I notice two orbs bobbing along upstream. At first I think they are basketballs that recent rains have washed out of some backyards bordering the creek. But as they drift closer, I realize that they are heads—talking heads! That is to say, they are disembodied heads, speaking to each other as they float. One head, I come to realize, belongs to John the Baptist, severed by Herod Antipas at the request of a spurned lover. The other belongs to Orpheus, severed by a band of angry Maenads in the hills of Thrace. We watch in stupefied silence as they pass us by.

ORPHEUS: These oaks! My friend, are you seeing these magnificent oaks?

JOHN: Your kin, I presume.

ORPHEUS: I was actually born from an alder tree, on a bank much like this one. But one day when I was walking in the woods, singing, I felt the shadow of something behind me. I turned and realized a stand of white oaks had wrenched their roots from the ground and were following the scent of my song.

JOHN: Neat trick.

ORPHEUS: Well, easy for a god.

JOHN: Half-god.

ORPHEUS: As you like.

JOHN: It was women that laid us low.

ORPHEUS: We represented the patriarchy. I think that's the term in use now.

JOHN: I was trying to overthrow the Roman patriarchy! I was trying to take back a stolen homeland.

ORPHEUS: You scared people with all that "offspring of vipers" talk. You had no music in your soul.

JOHN: A lot of good it did you.

ORPHEUS: But look how my scattered limbs have given birth to the bone-white branches of these sycamores.

JOHN: They do look oddly skeletal.

ORPHEUS: The entire earth is now endowed with my divinity.

JOHN: Settle down.

ORPHEUS: It was just a thought.

JOHN: One you stole from Pythagoras.

ORPHEUS: It's possible.

JOHN: What's that sound?

ORPHEUS: The wind blowing through a lyre. The one you can plainly see nailed to my head.

JOHN: I didn't want to ask.

ORPHEUS: It's alright. The Maenads did it after they killed me. Because I wouldn't teach them any of my songs.

JOHN: I think your patriarchy is showing.

ORPHEUS: Back then, I thought girls should only be backup singers. I was mistaken.

JOHN: Clearly. Have you heard Alicia Keys?

ORPHEUS: Yeah, she's great. A little overproduced, but still great.

JOHN: The fish aren't moving anymore.

ORPHEUS: It happens every time they hear this song. Hungry?

JOHN: Maybe later.

ORPHEUS: There's a poet who I think lives downstream from here. He says there are no unsacred places, only sacred places and desecrated places.

JOHN: You're thinking about the oaks again.

ORPHEUS: They were the basis of my alphabet—the consonants that the vowels passed through on the wind.

JOHN: Your alphabet was a lyric. Mine was a law.

ORPHEUS: Your wilderness was a desert. Mine was a forest.

JOHN: Meaning?

ORPHEUS: We brought back different laws. I wanted a bestiary, you wanted an avenging angel. You prophesized out of anger.

JOHN: It was for love of my people. You were not a Jew. You don't understand exile.

ORPHEUS: Tell me.

JOHN: My people wept by the rivers of Babylon. But our captors mocked us, demanded songs of joy. We hung our harps in the willows and refused. We could not sing our way home like you. Song failed us.

ORPHEUS: In the forest, song is reconciliation. It maps a path to the promised land.

JOHN: Which you no doubt think we are passing through now.

ORPHEUS: Passing through always.

JOHN: The fish have stopped swimming again.

ORPHEUS: Aren't they lovely?

JOHN: The sunfish look like tiny sunsets.

ORPHEUS: Yes, sunsets.

LILLIE LANGTRY—BRITISH ACTRESS, socialite, friend of Oscar Wilde—performed a daily ritual, weather permitting, of rolling naked in the morning dew. I've never quite shed enough clothes or inhibitions to try that, but when I take a thermos of coffee down to the creek in the morning, I do like to splash the cold water on my face. It's bracing, refreshing, and it always reminds me of that Tom T. Hall song "I Washed My Face in the Morning Dew." And since Hall has fallen out of fashion with the current country music crowd—producers of the sorriest nonsense to ever emanate from a car stereo— I think I'll just say some words about Kentucky's greatest songwriter. It's true, there are a lot of great contenders for that mantle—Jean Ritchie, Bill Monroe, Hazel Dickens, Dwight Yoakum, Ricky Skaggs, Loretta Lynn—and the distinction is by definition arbitrary, of course. But be that as it may, I'll go ahead and make my case based on three songs.

The first Tom T. Hall record I bought was *In Search of a Song*. I bought a lot more after that, but to me the first one was the best (and Hall himself agrees). In his autobiography *The Storyteller's Nashville*, Hall wrote, "I had simply exhausted all the 'I Love You' and 'You Are Cheating on Me' ideas that were in my head." So in the midseventies, he struck out on a road trip through Eastern Kentucky—in search of a song, or enough songs to make a record. Hall, whose mother died when he was eleven, had left his hometown of Olive Hill at age fifteen, after quitting school and working in a garment factory to support his father, who had been disabled by a hunting accident. He did a stint in the army, then headed to Nashville when he was discharged to get down to the serious business of writing songs. As a child back in Olive Hill, he had stared out at the dusty road that ran in front of his family's house and thought it bore "the promise of *elsewhere*." His ticket to Elsewhere, he decided, was a guitar. A young man named Lonnie Easterling taught him how to pick. That eventually got him to Nashville and to a fifty-dollar-a-week songwriting job. There he wrote "Hello Vietnam," a number one hit for Johnnie Wright, and started making some real money. In 1968, Jerry Kennedy at Mercury Records asked Hall if he wanted to make an LP of his own. With his flattop burr cut and ridiculously out-of-date clothes, Hall wasn't exactly the rhinestone cowboy type, and he certainly couldn't sing like a Glen Campbell.

But Mercury was in a bit of a lull, and Hall had written some damn good songs. For that first record, he wrote "I Washed My Face in the Morning Dew."

It's the tale of a man wandering from one "strange town" to another. In the first town, the county was hanging a man to no one's dismay. So the wanderer

> Washed my face in the morning dew,
> Bathed my soul in the sun,
> Washed my face in the morning dew
> And kept on movin' along.

In the second strange town, people were laughing at a "poor crippled man" begging for change. The wanderer washed his face in the morning dew and again moved on. The third strange town was peaceful and nice: the rich got richer and the poor got poorer, "and that just didn't seem right." Dew, face, move along. Back on the road, the wanderer imagined a future in which justice will eventually be served. And on he walked. It's a harrowing journey through the American landscape, one that seems to move chronologically from a 1940s lynching (Hall doesn't say the man is Black, but surely he is) to today's income gap, the widest in the developed world. What does it mean to wash one's face in the morning dew? In folk medicine, this daily ritual supposedly warded off skin blemishes. But in Hall's song, it was meant, as he wrote in his autobiography, to "purify your soul." To purify a country's soul.

The song was a minor hit. Hall bought a used tour bus from Loretta Lynn and became the most unlikely of country stars, writing and recording great songs like "That's How

I Got to Memphis," "Homecoming," and "Harper Valley
PTA." But after three decades in Elsewhere, Hall decided
it was time to head home to Eastern Kentucky. He called
up his writer friend Bill Littleton and proposed they hit
the road. Littleton would bring a camera, and Hall would
bring a notebook and a bottle of brandy. "I wanted to see,"
wrote Hall, "if anyone gave a damn about these people who
seemed so insignificant to the world in general."

In Search of a Song leads off with "The Year That
Clayton Delaney Died," an homage to Hall's first mentor,
Lonnie Easterling, who had died of TB at age nineteen. Hall
renamed Easterling after some neighbors, the Delaneys, who
lived on Clayton Hill. And it's true, the latter name scans
much better than the real one. And it's also true that "The
Year That Clayton Delaney Died" is the best song Hall ever
wrote, the best song almost anybody ever wrote. In it, Hall
remembers being a barefoot, eight-year-old kid who followed after "Clayton," Olive Hill's best guitar picker (in
that sense and many others, the song is a close cousin to
Ronnie Van Zant's "The Ballad of Curtis Loew"). In the
song, Clayton teaches the boy to play but warns him, "There
ain't no money in it / and it'll lead you to an early grave."
What else happens? The boy wonders why Clayton doesn't
take his talents to Tennessee. The boy's father explains that
Clayton is a drunk, and the boy remembers: "I can still see
him half-stoned pickin' out the 'Lovesick Blues.'" And then
Clayton dies. "Nobody ever knew it, but I went out in the
woods and I cried," remembers the narrator. But there in the
woods, he makes Clayton a promise: "I was gonna carry on
somehow / I'd give a hundred dollars if he could only see me

now." With its cantering tempo and stripped-down arrangement, the song offers a beautifully understated and unsentimental elegy to Easterling. However, it's not really a song that stands up to paraphrase; you'll have to go listen for yourself.

But while I'm still speaking in superlatives, I'll make one last claim: Hall's "Trip to Hyden" is the best song ever written about a mining disaster. Again, there's stiff competition here too, particularly Hazel Dickens's "The Mannington Mine Disaster," which simmers with a widow's righteous anger. On November 20, 1968, seventy-eight men were buried alive by a mine explosion outside the town of Mannington, West Virginia. To the mine owners, Dickens sings, "How can God forgive you, you do know what you've done. / You've killed my husband, now you want my son." "Trip to Hyden" takes place two years later, and a few days after the Hurricane Creek mine disaster, when on December 30, 1970, a blast killed thirty-eight men in a nonunion mine outside Hyden, Kentucky. The Bureau of Mines had declared the mine an "imminent danger" due to blasting hazards but allowed the mine to continue operating anyway. According to a *Louisville Courier-Journal* editor, one of the mine owners actually had the poor sense to stand at the mine site in the awful aftermath and complain about a mine safety bill that had passed a year earlier, after the Mannington explosion. Leslie County Judge George Wooton walked over and beat the man bloody, as he should have. Justice was done.

All of that happened a few days before Hall and Littleton arrived on the scene. Still, "Trip to Hyden" feels as much like journalism as it does a song. At one point, Hall even says of an undertaker, "Well I guess he thought we were reporters." And indeed, Hall doesn't sing the song so much as speak it over a simple, repeating guitar line. Like a good journalist, Hall observes, "Every half a mile a sign proclaimed that Christ was coming soon." But then he editorializes, "And I thought, 'Well, he'd sure be disappointed if he did.'" And like a journalist, Hall goes and talks with the locals: a couple that runs a café, then the sheriff, then an old man standing at the mouth of the mine—a man who is possibly the lone survivor of the blast because he tells Hall, "It was just like being right inside a shotgun." But Hall is surprised to see no sign of death there, just "mudholes and some junk." Then a woman at the site says the miners are worth more money dead then when "they's a-livin.'" To which Hall responds in the song's last line: "And I'll leave it there 'cause I suppose she told it pretty well."

There's a scene in Barbara Kopple's documentary *Harlan County USA* where an old miner, hacking with black lung as he speaks, tells a story about working in a deep mine alongside a mule that would haul out the coal the miner had loaded. A supervisor tells the miner to be careful and not let the mule stand under any timbers that might fall. The miner says, "Well, what about me? You concerned about my safety?" And the supervisor replies, "I can replace a man easier than I can replace a mule." That's what the woman at the end of the song meant.

Except for the line about Jesus, the song isn't political in any way. Yet it's hard to imagine any contemporary country artist, the ones they play on the radio, the ones that go to the CMA Awards, writing or singing anything remotely like it—a song about the tragedy of the working class. In his autobiography, Hall wrote that he hoped his fieldwork and the record that followed would encourage "others to say what they thought of being part of a life that was commonplace among country people." But of course that didn't happen, and now Tom T. Hall has been left behind, a relic of a time when a country song actually meant something.

SITTING BESIDE CLEAR Creek almost daily for the last few years, I have gradually come to believe that there are four basic ways of knowing, four epistemologies, if you will: the *ethical*, the *scientific*, the *aesthetic*, and the *spiritual*. That last mode is the slipperiest, and I will make no attempt to define it, since I believe anything we call the spirit exists beyond language and can only be known through each individual's intuitions. But intuitions are a way of knowing, even if they are not a way of speaking, or even thinking. We can know things in our bones that we can never adequately put into words. That lacunae I will leave as the inexplicable realm of the spirit. However, as a way of knowing, I think it lies in close proximity to the aesthetic. I think we would do well to consider the world not only as a naturalistic phenomenon but also as an *aesthetic* manifestation. To comprehend the world aesthetically is to see it through an artist's eyes and therefore to see it with more vividness, more texture, more light. A great religious painting, Giotto's *Joachim among the Shepherds*, for instance, draws us into its presence—the piercing blue sky, the sculptural mass of the tawny cliffs—so it can then release us back into a natural world that seems so much more intense for having been filtered through the alchemical lens of the aesthetic. That intensity of seeing and feeling is the spiritual understanding of the natural world that Giotto imparts through the aesthetic— through art. The trick in our everyday lives is to find a way to inflect our experience of the world with an aesthetic aura without having to visit an art museum or a cathedral first. This is easier to do when we are traveling because everything we see is new, which, I suppose, is why we love to travel—not just for the newness but for the aesthetic charge we get from the experience of moving through foreign places, seeing foreign things. Yet Thoreau famously said he traveled much in Concord. That is, he was able (as his voluminous journals show) to perform the unusual feat of seeing the common as always new and strange, to see the ordinary as extraordinary. The enemies of the aesthetic are neither the practical nor the intellectual, wrote John Dewey in his brilliant book *Art as Experience*: "They are the humdrum." Nothing to Thoreau ever looked or felt humdrum.

Many readers have complained that the later portions of Thoreau's journals shift from the aesthetic and the spiritual to the drably scientific, to observation without insight. But I think that move is an understandable one. One rarely learns about the nucleated cell in a biology class and becomes inspired to go explore the woods in search of the eukaryotic beauty of slime molds. But to stumble upon the spidery luminescence of a slime mold (the name belies the thing) might nudge one to start thinking about the origins of this single-cell organism. That's the move from the aesthetic to the scientific. With wonder, we gaze up at the night sky under a

new moon and suddenly find ourselves wanting to understand the movement of the constellations, the phases of the
moon. And of course it isn't only the beautiful and the sublime that pull us in the direction of explanation, of science.
The catastrophe of climate change has forced millions of
us to get schooled in the details of a changing atmosphere,
a changing ocean, a changing landscape. Understanding
this science then pushes us, or should push us, into the final
mode of knowing, the ethical. Again, John Dewey can be
our guide here. For that incomparable American philosopher, science wasn't just a set of facts to be memorized; it
was a method of critical inquiry, "an habitual disposition
of mind." The nature of science is to ask: (1) What do we
know? (2) How do we know what we know? (3) How do we
know what we know is actually true? To answer these questions, we investigate, analyze data, conduct experiments,
engage in peer review. Dewey believed that sound, unbiased
scientific inquiry would lead to sound value judgments and
sound decision-making. That decision-making would then
lead to sound actions. "Science must have something to say
about *what* we do, and not merely about *how* we may do
it," he wrote. His example was the warship. Science led to
its invention, but the aims of the warship in our society are,
he said, a holdover of barbarism. That is to say, a particular,
violent value system led to the warship, whereas in Dewey's
philosophy, the science would come first, and that scientific
inquiry would lead to a more humane value system than
the one that produced the warship. How? For one, we can
call for future action based on the science, not on bias. The
call for action concerning climate change is obviously much

different when it is based on science instead of a mere belief in the good of endless economic growth. Secondly, we can *test* the values and the actions that follow from the science. Do those values and actions lead to decreases in atmospheric CO_2 or do they lead to more fires, heat waves, and hurricanes? Thus, scientific inquiry improves our ability to make ethical decisions. That was the core of John Dewey's version of participatory democracy.

But as recent political upheavals have shown, 35 to 40 percent of Americans do not believe in Dewey's method of inquiry or his democratic future. They do not believe in climate change or evolution or empirically proven election results. They live inside their own science-proof religious, cultural, and economic mythologies. In short, they live in an anti-intellectual, anti-scientific realm that, if left unchecked, will put an end to this country's democratic experiment. What's more, this skewed thinking may very well lead us into a violent, desperate, uninhabitable future. I am not optimistic. But I do believe there is at least a *way* forward, based on these four modes of knowing. In our daily lives, there is a way to move fluidly around this quadratic equation—from the aesthetic to the spiritual, from the scientific to the ethical, from the aesthetic to the scientific, from the spiritual to the ethical—and every other of the twenty-four movements inherent in this quadrant. Whether we choose that way is an entirely different question.

THE POST THAT holds up one corner of our deck is beginning to sag alarmingly. So I do what I always do in times of country crisis: I call my neighbor Jim Maffett. In the winter when my pipes freeze, Jim comes over in coveralls, unscrews the particle board under the house, and shows me the exact pipe to which we need to apply the flame of our propane blowtorches. Today, Jim comes over with a homemade prop built out of two-by-fours and slowly muscles the supporting outer beam back to its original height. I redig the hole around the post and mix concrete in a wheelbarrow.

"Listen to that," Jim says. I listen. "A cuckoo and a wood thrush. That's the sound of summer right there."

I don't know anyone who pays closer attention to the workings of the natural world than my two friends named Jim—Maffett and Krupa. "Look at that," says the former as he points to the ground a few feet from where we're working. Something small and brownish is moving in the grass. We draw closer. "It's a wolf spider," Jim says. "See, she's got all of her babies on her back." And astonishingly enough, the dorsal side of her abdomen *is* covered in what looks to be about fifty tiny spiderlings. She'll carry them around for several weeks until they're old enough to hunt for themselves. We don't think of spiders hunting, but the wolf spider earns its moniker by eschewing the usual spider web and instead sprinting after its prey on the ground. With eight menacing eyes and venomous fangs, the wolf spider must seem a true terror to any insect about to experience the last few seconds of its life before being liquefied by venom. All this Jim explains to me before we get back to the more banal work of saving my deck from its own demise.

I've never met an American male quite like Jim. He is just as at home in the woods as he is in his shop rebuilding classic motorcycles, and he has an encyclopedic knowledge of both the natural and the mechanical world. Along with his wife, Lisa, he moved up here thirty-five years ago and set about learning everything he could about the place. He can name every tree, every wildflower, every bird, every insect. He can build a house, which he did for a living, and as a trained instructor, he has led groups scuba diving throughout the Caribbean. He is far better read than most English grad students, and he certainly reads more broadly. But like other men I've met with little formal education, he is self-effacing and often dismissive of his vast body of knowledge. "Hell, I'm barely literate," he'll say if someone expresses amazement at some natural phenomenon—say the genetic history of the water lily—he has just explained. Once, I told him he was an autodidact, and he said, "I'll have to go look that up later." But he knew exactly what it meant. In fact, Jim Maffett and Jim Krupa are probably the two smartest men I know, or have ever known. Their secret, I think, is simply a relentless curiosity about the world and how it works. When future global temperatures careen beyond two degrees Celsius and the real shitstorm starts, Melissa and I could survive for quite some time as long as the two Jims are around. Krupa could kill and dress any animal in North America, and Maffett could build and rebuild us a respectable compound out of baling wire and a set of pliers.

Now Jim Maffett places a thick cardboard mold around the post, and I fill it with cement. With the new footer in place, we backfill the hole with gravel.

"Come up to the garden later," Jim says, "and I'll show you our monarch operation in full swing."

Jim and Lisa maintain the kind of garden that appears,

and has appeared, in magazines. Perennials and annuals mix together around a koi pond, water fountains, and an outdoor tiki bar. When I arrive, Jim is snipping inch-square pieces from milkweed leaves and placing each one in a small plastic container, the kind that usually hold condiments in restaurants. Why is he doing this? Because over the last twenty years, 90 percent of the world's monarch butterfly population has vanished. Migrating throngs that once spread across forty-five acres of oyamel trees in Michoacán, Mexico, now only occupy 1.7 acres. The main culprit, unsurprisingly, is the Roundup herbicide that midwestern farmers have sprayed on their soybean and corn fields to eradicate anything that isn't soybeans or corn, including milkweed—the only thing monarchs will eat. Suburbanization of farmland has also played a part. "I've watched it happen over the years," Jim says. "Wild milkweed gets eaten up by subdivisions or horse farms or whatever. They always get rid of the milkweed." Since 1999, 97 percent of the milkweed in the United States has been eradicated. Plus, illegal logging in Mexico is wiping out the only place monarchs winter, outside of a few eucalyptus groves around Monterey, California. And climate change is also playing a role. Because of warmer temperatures, the monarchs are migrating earlier, only to arrive in the States to find the milkweed plant hasn't leafed out yet.

Since even in ideal conditions, a monarch egg has about a 10 percent chance of becoming a butterfly due to predation and parasitism, Jim and Lisa, along with thousands of other Americans, plant red and orange zinnias—colors monarchs can't resist. Next to the zinnias, Jim has raised a stand of milkweed he transplanted from the edge of a local farm. "The guy looked at me like I had three heads when I asked if I could dig it up," Jim says.

The relocated plants are thriving now. Jim turns over each leaf to have a look at the gray-green undersides. Sure enough, almost every leaf has one tiny white egg attached to it. "They only lay one per leaf," Jim says, "so the baby caterpillar will have plenty to eat when it hatches." It's the alkaloid chemical makeup of the milkweed plant that makes the monarch so distasteful to birds. That's one evolutionary strategy for staying alive; another is mimicry, which the viceroy butterfly has used to make itself look identical to the monarch.

When the pollen-size egg hatches, the first thing the microscopic larva does is eat its own egg. Then it sets to work devouring its home leaf. This is where Jim steps in to save the caterpillar from birds, spiders, dragonflies, and worst of all perhaps, tachinid flies. Like the *Glyptapanteles* wasp that shook Darwin's belief in a benevolent God, the tachinid female lays her eggs on caterpillars, and then those tiny parasites feed off their host, eventually killing it. Farmers first imported the tachinid fly from Asia as a natural pesticide: it eats caterpillars that eat their crops. But the tachinid fly has been bad for monarchs. So Jim puts the larvae in the small containers until they are large enough to transfer into a netted enclosure, which sits in the shade on his porch. We go over to take a look. At the bottom of the cage, inch-long caterpillars are feeding on the leaves Jim has picked. As larvae, they will gain 2,700 times their original weight. They will go through several stages of "instar," where their skin splits open and a larger larva emerges. Finally, the caterpillar, whose black, white, and yellow banding runs horizontally across its body, climbs to the top of the cage where it hangs like a *J* from a silk thread. Then, when the final instar molt takes place, a bright green, podlike being emerges: the chrysalis. In essence, one animal has turned completely into another one. And inside that second is a third, a fully formed monarch butterfly. "That just blows my mind," says Jim.

The next day, I return to see the caterpillar has pulled on the green armor of its chrysalis, or rather it has burst its final skin to reveal a smooth green capsule dotted with gold flecks and capped with an acorn-like cupule. Over the next week, the caterpillar will completely liquefy, using its own digestive enzymes; that is, it will eat itself alive before reconstituting that bag of puss into a winged creature.

Ten days later, Jim calls and says come quick if I want to see the miracle. When I arrive at his shop, the chrysalis is black and shimmering. Over the next hour, we watch the bottom of this pupa slowly crack open. The proboscis emerges first, then a head, then the antennae. Then suddenly, there's the flash of orange wings, and a fully formed monarch clings with its legs to the now empty and transparent chrysalis. It's like watching a hammer turn into a hacksaw—right as you were reaching for the hammer.

Just as monarchs go through four stages in one life cycle, they also experience four generations in one year. In February or March, the migratory monarchs come out of hibernation in Mexico, look for a mate, then head north to lay the eggs of the first generation. With the 1,200- to

1,800-mile journey and the fertilization completed, the females lay their eggs, then die. The stages of life for the first generation only last for about six weeks. Another generation follows in May, and then the third gestates in July. The forth iteration, called the Methuselah generation, will live for up to ten months, long enough to fly to the state of Michoacán in the Sierra Nevada of Mexico, hibernate over the winter, then fly back here to lay eggs and die.

"It's just amazing to me," Jim says, "to think that one butterfly's great-grandkids are the ones that go back to where they came from." They alight from Kentucky, and somehow they know where to go. "And you got millions that go there, all trying to find the same spot," says Jim.

He knows his efforts aren't really going to help much. A far better solution would be to stop cutting or spraying the millions of miles of US highways and let them grow up as wildlife habitat. Or convince farmers to leave a border of their fields clean of herbicides. But there's little chance of that happening. The monarch will probably follow the one million species also on their way to extinction over the next few decades. And *Homo sapiens*, mostly, couldn't care less. But we will be the lesser for it. By diminishing the world, we will diminish ourselves until we are finally scavenging through the burnt-out ruins of our own arrogance, our self-centeredness, perhaps our own impending extinction.

I—THIS MOMENTARY ACCUMULATION of particles, this confederacy of microbes, floating in a saline sea—wake this morning to a composition in gray: gray sky, gray trees, gray rocks, all blurred out of focus by a gray fog. After I get the

dogs and chickens fed, I disappear down among the sycamores and let the fog erase my own shaky outlines. It's as if
I'm moving through a painting by J. M. W. Turner or an
essay by William James, who said we should think of the self
as a verb—an enactment, not an entity. *Selving.* I like that
idea. Or maybe we should think of the self as something like
Clear Creek, an enactment *and* an entity. The creek is always
and never the same, a million years old and reborn every
second, a continuous sentence constantly writing its autobiography on these limestone walls.

We are, of course, a country drowning in self. We are surrounded by an entire consumer culture that depends for its
survival on our self-consciousness, our self-doubt, our self-
loathing. Which turns all of this so-called narcissism into
the opposite of the original Greek meaning: self-love. But
I have a slightly different take on the traditional reading of
the myth of Narcissus. When the beautiful youth bent over
a stream to drink, I don't believe it was his own reflection
with which he fell in love. I think he did see that visage and
then looked through it to the pebbles, grasses, and darters
below. And so it was the entire natural world that entranced
Narcissus, and he came to understand everything in it as
part of himself and he as part of it. He escaped a shallow
narcissism of the small, individual self to discover a larger,
ecological self that erased the boundaries of the body, the
boundaries of the ego. That was the true self from which he
could not turn away.

In his Phi Beta Kappa address of 1837, "The American
Scholar," Ralph Waldo Emerson said that the first allegiance of "Man Thinking" is to nature because "its beauty

is the beauty of his own mind. Its laws are the laws of his own mind." Like the Stoics' mantra, *zen kata physin*—"live according to nature"—Emerson saw a precise correlation between soil and soul, the outer nature and the inner landscape. Like James, he replaced the static, Platonic self with something much more expansive and fluid. Thus, he contended that the maxim inscribed on the Temple to Apollo at Delphi, "Know thyself," was really interchangeable with his own precept: "Study nature." Like his friends Walt Whitman and Henry David Thoreau, Emerson was building a bridge (Whitman chose the symbol of the transcontinental railroad) from the Western to the Eastern mind. Specifically, we might say he was reaching toward the thirteenth-century Buddhist teacher Dōgen Zenji, who said, "To study the self is to forget the self. To forget the self is to be enlightened by all things." That's a long way from Socrates, who in the *Phaedo* couldn't even see the tree he was sitting under, so obsessed was he with the narrowly examined self.

About fifteen years ago, I met a Zen master who instructed his students (I wasn't one of them) that they should bow—to everything. Dae Gak, the Zen master, traced his spiritual lineage back to a famous monk from the Tang dynasty, Seon Do Sunim, who said that since "everything is Buddha," everything deserves a bow. To bow to a stand of pawpaw trees means acknowledging some symbiotic connection to them, as in my own myth of Narcissus. In bowing, we are reminded that the self is larger than the body's own fortress. Dae Gak might say (and an evolutionary biologist would agree) that because we share some psychological or genetic kinship with all of life, we are in some inscrutable way bowing *to ourselves* or perhaps even to our ultimate, original *self*. Dae Gak calls this the "unborn, undifferentiated mind." Poets and mystics have called it the face we had before we were born. All of which is to say, it really has no name. It is the one that becomes the many, the many who then go in search of the one. And bowing, perhaps, becomes a way back to that reconciliation. In bowing, says Dae Gak, you see the error of self-centered activity. I've found this to be true. For one thing, you feel slightly foolish doing it. At least at first. But that's the ego, the part of ourselves that cares how others perceive us, thinking that way. And it is precisely this ego that the bowing is meant to defuse, subvert, lay low. It is the ego that stands in the way of recognizing a larger version of the self, of seeing some shared substance between you and other living things. Bowing breaks down the wall between subject and object, self and other. It opens a space through which each can pass into the other so that there *is no object*, only a constellation of other subjects.

I practice bowing now as the fog is lifting down by the creek. I bow to a twisted cedar. Then I bow to a box turtle slowly crossing the trail. Finally, I bow to the creek—that other self. It feels good. It feels like a kind of release, a release from petty insecurities and anxious masquerades. Each bow feels like an exhalation, a letting go of any fixed notions of the self. I feel a sense of reverence that then turns into a feeling of humility. I am no longer, like the classical Greek artists, obsessed with my own human form, but rather, like the ancient painters of the Chinese Tang dynasty, I sense my own body becoming thankfully diminished in the presence of these woods, this gorge. The bowing feels like a supplication that has nothing to do with worship, with the heretical pantheism my grandfather would have seen in this gesture. Dualities begin to fall away. I even begin to sense a blurring of the line between life and death. There is certainly no better place than the woods, with its fallen trees and leaf-shredding beetles, to understand how death feeds back into life in an endless transformation of substance into substance. None of that scares me now as I continue to slowly bow. I begin to breathe deeper, slower. When I straighten up, I feel like a gray cloud has cleared from my mind. I feel like I have shed a small part of my Western inheritance and now realize that finding and losing oneself might in fact be the same thing.

A DARK CLOUD of blackbirds, about a hundred of them, descend on the creek to drink from the banks. The last flags of summer are falling from the oxeye sunflower. The season's final wildflower, the crooked-stem aster, is blooming in thin soil and talus at the base of steep outcrops. Some even grow in the clefts of limestone walls high above the creek. I take up my usual position on the nuptial rock. Falling sycamore leaves are beginning to clot the riffles, which are now only a trickle because of the dry September. And so there's a rare quiet. Upstream, a fawn struggles across the creek behind its mother, nose barely reaching above the surface. To my right, box elders lean over the water. When I glance into the shade of the shallows, looking for the giant snapping turtle I saw here earlier in the summer, I see instead the lifeless body of a thick green caterpillar. I fish out the three-inch larva and hold it in my palm. The body, covered in a fine white hair, is still warm, soft, bloated. Eight yellow spots—spiracles—dot each segment of its abdomen, and four tiny yellow horns poke out of its head. It must have fallen out of the higher branches of the box elder and drowned. I set the caterpillar down on the boulder and begin to sketch its corpse in my notebook. When I'm finished, I decide to wrap the insect in a sycamore leaf and take it up to the house for identification. Just then I notice the head raise up slightly from the abdomen. I poke the caterpillar gently with my pen, thinking this must be some form of rigor mortis. But after a few more minutes, the head and the tail both lift a couple of centimeters. Then its thoracic segments lengthen slightly. Slowly, the caterpillar rolls onto its yellow legs. Then its whole body becomes a series of undulations that eventually double its length. This wave that passes through the caterpillar propels it into a sluggish forward motion that begins at its sturdy anal prolegs and pulses all the way to its head. The larva manages about an inch per minute as it traverses the long stretch of limestone, heading home to the box elder. Its white hairs glisten in the sun. Crouching on my knees to watch this deliberate journey, I feel my mind slowing to the pace of this Lazarus-like insect. I grow determined to see where this passage leads. But when the caterpillar reaches the edge of the rock, its whole body seems to become a confused antenna that reaches fruitlessly in all directions for some kind of contact, some traction. Tentatively, it touches the lobe of a dead leaf, then draws back onto the rock. Finally, I place the end of my wooden walking stick at the ledge in question, and with some hesitation, the caterpillar, which I later learn is the larva of the imperial moth, shimmies onto the shaft. I delicately transfer the stick to the base of the tree, where I brush aside a clump of dead leaves and find, clinging upside-down to a slender green shoot, another larva of the same species. I've never seen this caterpillar in my life, and now I've seen two within an hour. Could this be its mate? I wonder for a second before coming rather obtusely to the realization that caterpillars don't have mates; they are simply the leaf-eating stage between the egg and the pupa that will finally crack open to expose a newly winged creature. Still, though not a mate in any reproductive sense, when I twirl the caterpillar off of my stick at the base of the new shoot, the second larva does crawl down from its post and actually passes beneath the abdominal segments of my own foundling. Together, the two proceed together over mosses and lichens, up toward the tree's leafy canopy. I watch until both are out of sight.

WHEN THE GREEK philosopher Thales was asked why he had no kids of his own, he replied it was because he loved children.

IT'S EARLY SEPTEMBER, when wild chicory and ironweed crowd the roadsides and ditches. At the top of our lane, I frighten a young raccoon who doesn't notice me until I am fifteen feet away. It lunges for a young hickory tree and scampers up to glower down at me. When I take a few steps toward the tree, the raccoon claws its way higher until the branches are too thin to hold its weight. As if launching from a springboard, the raccoon dives into another tree further down the slope. All around us, the thick, spiky husks of the buckeye trees are splitting open to drop their brown nuts all over the lane where I walk in the evenings. Each night, I toss the ones that haven't already been crushed by tires down into the woods. But I also pick up a couple of these seeds and just roll them around in my right hand. They do look like large brown eyeballs that have been peeled from the sockets—I suppose this is where they get their name—of bucks. Or any large ungulate really. I like to think of the thousands of these smooth orbs, hanging and falling now, as the eyes of the forest. When I get home, I drop the two buckeyes in a green-tinted Ball jar. When the jar is full, it looks like a collection of disembodied eyes, and I like to watch them watching me from the kitchen windowsill. I don't feel too bad that I've removed them from their native ground or from the task they were born for—germination. For one thing, our west-facing slope is covered with ample buckeye trees already. It seems an unlikely victory for such a shrubby plant, but I would estimate buckeyes make up 40 percent of that hillside's arboreal population. Perhaps by entombing in glass these few seeds, I'm giving a coffee tree or a yellowwood the chance to find some soil and sunlight. Forests thrive best when their populations are diverse because diseases have a harder time taking hold (and so do loggers, for that matter). But beyond that, what all these buckeye seeds represent is the absolute profligacy of nature.

Three hundred and sixty million years ago, plants invented seeds as a way to reproduce. The chinquapin and white oaks that spread throughout this gorge will each produce over a million seeds in a mast year. Or consider

Kentucky's state tree, *Liriodendron tulipifera*, the tulip poplar. Two million years after the evolution of seeds, flowers came on the scene as a way to flag down pollinators and call them into nature's great exchange. The tulip poplar actually heats its flowers, seducing beetles to spend cool spring nights inside the petals' white walls. It's a cozy boudoir where beetles are often known to copulate; then at dawn, they emerge covered in pollen to unknowingly help the poplar along with its own sexual designs. Every species gets something for its effort in this elaborate orchestration of enlightened self-interest, conducted by the hidden hand of natural selection.

What is the lesson here? That trees behave nothing like mammals when it comes to reproduction and the rearing of offspring. They can't after all; they've got these roots that pretty much curtail anything other than asexual reproduction. The alternative is to scatter seeds all over creation, carried on the wind, the water, the backs of bees and bears, in the bellies of birds. It's scattershot, the opposite of efficiency, and some trees actually die from exhaustion after their sexual season. But most have found a way to make it work, mainly through cooperation with other species. Though nature *is* red in tooth and claw, as the owls around here can attest, there is also great cooperation within a woodland community. To speak in Darwin's terms, the *fittest* for survival are often those species that choose to cooperate through a symbiotic existence, through coevolution. As for the buckeye trees, hummingbirds and long-tongued bees pollinate their flowers in exchange for nectar. Every species gets something for its effort: the animals get sugar and the trees get a chance to spread their gamete to another buckeye on down the hill in this elaborate orchestration of enlightened self-interest, conducted by the hidden hand of natural selection.

Recent research, particularly that of Suzanne Simard, has begun to bear this out. Simard's studies in British Columbia have shown how mycorrhizas—partnerships between trees and fungi—have created unfathomably intricate, symbiotic networks. The fungi fuse with tree roots, extracting water, phosphorus, and nitrogen from the soil in exchange for carbon-rich sugars the trees make through photosynthesis. Indeed, fungal threads can link nearly every tree in a forest, even different species. In one experiment, Simard stripped Douglas fir seedlings of their leaves, leaving them to die. The seedlings sent stress signals, along with some carbon encouragement, to nearby ponderosa pines, which then accelerated their production of defensive enzymes. Simard even found that if a tree is about to die, it will sometimes bequeath its remaining carbon to arboreal neighbors. Trees, it turns out, have their own social network, and just as with humans, their survival depends as much on cooperation—perhaps much more—as it does on competition. Like humans (when humans are behaving), they engage in reciprocity, fair exchange. Simard has even compared the trees, plants, fungi, and microbes of a forest to a superorganism—one symbiotic whole made of many different parts.

The maverick biologist Lynn Margulis argued this for many decades before Simard was old enough to begin her research. Margulis coined the term *symbiogenesis* to explain the creation of new life from old through a symbiotic relationship. Her most famous example is the nucleated cell. Two thousand billion years ago, free-floating bacteria formed a federation with a capital (the nucleus) and a border (the cell membrane) that became the origin of "higher" life forms. "In short," Margulis writes, "I believe that most evolutionary novelty arose, and still arises, directly from symbiosis." Cooperation, argues Margulis and Simard, is the name of the game. It was Herbert Spencer, not Charles Darwin, who first coined the term "survival of the fittest." When Darwin borrowed it for later editions of *The Origin of Species*, he never deployed it as survival of the physically strongest and most violent. For Darwin, fitness simply meant fecundity. Survival is not, or does not have to be, a zero-sum game of winners and losers. It can be a *non*-zero-sum game; Margulis gives the example of children playing house. In a famous case study, political scientist Robert Axelrod convened game theorists, mathematicians, and evolutionary biologists to play a non-zero-sum game called the Prisoner's Dilemma. Participants would get three points for cooperating, one point for defecting, and five points for defecting while others cooperated. A Machiavellian approach would therefore seem the best way to win—convince others to cooperate while you take advantage of them. But it turned out that greedy and bullying participants were consistently the worst performers, while cooperators moved on to the next round. Axelrod then sped up the game through computer models and found that after many "generations," hardly any of the ruthless players survived. In a non-zero-sum game, cooperation increases over time. Good begets good. Margulis summarized the results to say Axelrod's work was consistent with her views "that all large organisms came from smaller prokaryotes [non-nucleated cells] that together won a victory for cooperation, for the art of mutual living."* It's also interesting to recall that initially, both Margulis's and Simard's work was rejected as too "soft," too "motherly." But the research on cooperation became too impressive to dismiss. Cooperation finally, belatedly, had its day.

TONIGHT I DISCOVER nine luna moths affixed to the inside screen door of our back porch. Due to our dogs' helpless impulse to go charging through the lower screens after squirrels and house wrens, our porch is admittedly porous. Still, I am startled to walk out at dusk and find the door covered in these papery creatures. They are a green glory, with their large, fanlike wings fringed in purple and stamped by evolution with two black and gold eyespots to fool predators. The great taxonomist Linnaeus thought the spots looked like moons—though decidedly hooded moons—and pronounced them lunar. These nine moths are about to complete their life cycle by laying up to six hundred eggs on the leaves of the walnuts and hickories that surround this porch. Those eggs will hatch and go through five instars. Then the larva will spin a cocoon, wrap it in leaves for camouflage, then drop to the ground and begin the great transformation from pupa to flying moth. When ready, the adults

---

* The leading evolutionary biologist Richard Dawkins once wrote of Axelrod's book *The Evolution of Cooperation*, "The world's leaders should all be locked up with this book and not released until they have read it. This would be a pleasure to them and might save the rest of us. *The Evolution of Cooperation* deserves to replace the Gideon Bible."

will cut their way out of the cocoon using serrated spurs on their thorax. They usually emerge in the mornings so their wings can dry during the day, and by nighttime, the moths are here on my screen, ready to mate, lay eggs, and die. In fact, since I've been watching, four of the moths have commenced copulating, with the males hovering above the females like one side of a fluttering hinge. Of the 160,000 species of moths in the world, the *Actias luna* is incomparably beautiful. I've known this for many years, but I've never seen a quorum together like this, glowing in the soft light of the porch.

Is their beauty, like that of the sunfish, an adaptive trait? It is obviously compelling to the human eye and presumably is to other members of the species. Scientists call such distinctive coloration an amatory signal. It certainly makes them easy to find, though the female also gives off a pheromone that the male can track for miles. But their size also makes luna moths conspicuous—even with their leaf-colored green wings—to owls, as scattered moth wings on the forest floor attest. Like the male peacock's tale, their beautiful eyespots attract unwanted, as well as wanted, attention (and nothing frustrated Darwin more than his inability to explain the male peacock). But the evolutionary answer for both moth and peacock seems to be that the point of their existence *isn't* survival but simply reproduction. *That* is the real worldwide drive in all five kingdoms of life: bacteria, protists, fungi, plants, and animals. If we need any more evidence, we can just consider one last detail about the luna moth: it has no mouth. Since the insect will only live one week in this, its final, flourishing manifestation, there is no point. The point is only copulation, fertilization, and colonization—finding six hundred leaves in seven days to start the life cycle all over again. Knowing this, I decide to make a tall drink and spend a long while out on the porch, basking in the fleeting presence of these evanescent creatures.

I HAVE SPENT the adult part of my life shedding the calcified layers of belief that built up and became painfully encrusted during childhood. And I have gradually chiseled down to one final piece of bedrock. That is to say, I think I can abdicate every religious precept except for one—my seemingly inextricable belief that a creator exists and *is* the creation. The earliest philosophical question was, Why is there something instead of nothing? My own mind simply can't fathom that something *could* come from nothing. There must have always been some substance. But even if the astrophysicists are right and the universe did come into being 13.7 billion years ago, I still find myself falling back on Spinoza's idea that the universe is *causa sui*, self-born, and thus of one substance: God-or-Nature. In the preamble to the Declaration of Independence, Thomas Jefferson wrote that our inherent human rights are written in "the laws of Nature and of Nature's God." The founding fathers were mainly Deists, which is to say pantheists—Nature's God becomes synonymous with God-or-Nature. To "love" this impersonal God is very different from the love Christians profess for the personal God of their Bible. Instead, what this amounts to is a belief in the God we find in the book of Job—the one I can know nothing about except what I perceive in the natural world. As the voice in the whirlwind told Job, it is folly and hubris to think that we can know the image, the mind, the intentions of God. It is foolish to think of God as a "father" who wants certain things for us and prohibits others. This is such a *diminishing* of the God we see dramatized in Job's litany of nature's divine emanations. Rather, to most revere God, we must admit that we know nothing of God—except what we know through silent supplications and through the study of nature. For me, what it all comes down to is this: one can say that the natural world is completely material or one can say the natural world is completely divine—and it is exactly the same statement.

INSECTS HAVE STRIPPED all the bark from an ash tree and written a wandering hieroglyphic into the white trunk that now stands like a sibylline totem pole. I suspect they are scripting our own demise, writing a withering elegy for a species that spoke only hollow allegiance to courage, justice, and mercy.

A GOLDFINCH PLUCKS the last seeds from the sunflowers leaning over the garden fence. With its leaves wilting away, the okra looks like planted javelins in this autumn light. These eight plants have been dependable producers through the last two months. But now, the last fruit forms a single spearhead at the top of each thick green stalk, and what was once a brilliant yellow flower with a deep scarlet pistil is now a shriveled brown husk at the tip of each green spear. I have to bend down each stalk to reach the final pods with my pruning shears, but I harvest just enough for one final summer side dish.

Walking the trail beside the creek this morning, I find fanned out all around a dead stump the bright orange and yellow clusters of an edible bracket fungus called sulfur shelf. When I return in the afternoon with a pocketknife and a paper bag, I cut away the most tender growth. Back at the house, I slice the wide caps into one-inch pieces and fry them in oil and garlic. Melissa is talking on the phone to her twin sister in California.

"Tell her there's a fungus among us," I say from the stove.

Melissa covers the phone and replies, "I'm not going to tell her that."

The local name for this mushroom is "chicken of the woods," and after about ten minutes in a cast iron skillet, it does have the taste and it even possesses the consistency of chicken.

I assure Melissa that these fungi aren't poisonous, but then for some reason I launch into a mini-lecture about a mushroom in Appalachia called the Angel of Death because, if eaten, it will make one's inner throat swell to the point of asphyxiation in half an hour. Midway through my soliloquy, I can tell it was badly timed. Melissa begins an internet search for *Laetiporus sulphureus*. "You say they're not poisonous, but it says here don't eat them with more than one glass of wine."

"Well, we aren't having any wine," I point out. "Just try one."

I fork a piece over to her, but I can tell she isn't that impressed.

"Don't they taste like chicken?" I say.

"I was hoping they would taste like mushrooms," she replies.

This is to be the last meal from our garden this year, but I can tell it isn't off to a propitious start. I try to redeem things with what remains of the basil and green tomatoes. I mix up some pesto and fry the tomatoes along with the okra.

I set this vegetable combination on our blue plates spun by a local potter. Melissa takes a picture to post online and I feel vindicated.

"That okra's del-ic-io-so," she says between bites. She's right. My mother grew up in South Georgia; I know how to fry okra.

"Great job with the pesto too." Melissa steers clear of the mushrooms. That's alright. She will take over the cooking duties for the rest of the year, distrustful of me with more complicated autumn fare. That suits me fine. I'm proud of my small summer harvest and have almost forgotten the cabbage and kale I lost to aphids and cabbage worms. Next year, I promise myself, I'll be more diligent, more attentive to their attacks. But for now, I feel like celebrating my modest garden accomplishments up in the confines of Pairidaeza.

"Since you didn't eat your mushrooms," I say, "how about a little wine on the back porch?"

"How about you give me a little smooch first?"

It's ELECTION DAY, the only day when we Americans enjoy any semblance of autonomy in controlling the direction of this country. I drive into Nonesuch to mark my ballot at our small fire station. The station's two trucks are outside gleaming in the sun, and a very short line waits to approach the two voting stations inside. I am thinking, as I often do on Election Day, about this poem by Vachel Lindsay:

Why I Voted the Socialist Ticket
I am unjust, but I can strive for justice.
My life's unkind, but I can vote for kindness.
I, the unloving, say life should be lovely.
I, that am blind, cry out against my blindness.

Man is a curious brute—he pets his fancies—
Fighting mankind, to win sweet luxury.
So he will be, though law be clear as crystal,
Tho' all men plan to live in harmony.

Come, let us vote against our human nature,
Crying to God in all the polling places
To heal our everlasting sinfulness
And make us sages with transfigured faces.

There has never been an American poet quite like Vachel Lindsay. He was a nineteenth-century traveling bard, a knight-errant, a wild man of the heartland who, through his poetry, campaigned for "beauty, democracy and civilization." He was an early champion of African American and Native American art forms. On the road, he often traded his poetry pamphlets for food and shelter. He took up the causes of the abused and the dispossessed, singing his poems in a jarring, syncopated fashion (often beating a conga drum) that left him unfashionable in the staid circles of far less adventurous poetry. As with many American originals, the country had little room for Vachel Lindsay.

If I had more of his moxie, I would recite this poem right now to those standing in line with me, and they would know that I too am going to vote for the socialist candidate. And for exactly the same reasons Lindsay did. Ever since Eugene Debs was incarcerated for leading railroad strikes, then emerged from prison as a socialist and a presidential candidate in the 1900 election, we have been hearing that socialism is unrealistic, too idealistic against the hoarding capitalist soul of human nature. Which is what I love about Lindsay's poem; it allows for all that and votes for the socialist anyway. The poem says a vote should be an aspiration for the country, not a confirmation of inevitable corruption and complaisance. We can still strive to be better than we are. We can vote for the person who still believes in such a thing, in such a future. We can reject a nasty and brutish "human nature" that only affirms the fortunes of those who believe in it. We can reject the idea that Darwin's theory of "the fittest" only applies to the strongest, the most brutal, the most self-serving. If we do not cry to God in all the polling places to heal our sins, we can at least still vote for a set of values and beliefs that might "make us sages with transfigured faces."

I'M PERCHED ON the nuptial rock in the late afternoon of a warm October day. Around my chair, the tips of a fallen cherry leaf have curled up like the stem and stern of a tiny gondola. When I blow the leaf off this rock, out over the creek, it does indeed land on its keel and, rudderless, spins downstream without taking on a drop of water. What army of red ants might charter this autumn *Argo* to carry its crew further and faster to the next campaign? Surely my own obstreperous ancestors, the Norwegian Vikings, must have studied this modest leaf when they began to build the world's first seaworthy warships. The primary vein showed them how to set the keel while the perpendicular secondary veins told them where to space the frames. It's obvious when you think about it.

One of the most fundamental differences, it seems to me, between the Eastern and the Western mind is that here in the West, we've almost always assumed that the natural world has nothing to teach us. We treat it as dead matter—a "resource" at best and a demonic backdrop at worse. The West's first surviving literary work, *The Epic of Gilgamesh*, begins with the hero embarking on a journey to, in the name of immortality, cut down the trees on Cedar Mountain and slay the forest spirit, Huwawa. We have been clear-cutting forests ever since. India's national poet, Rabindranath Tagore, made a compelling distinction between Eastern and Western literature, and it too has to do with ships and trees. A central motif in Western literature, argued Tagore, is man's fight with the sea, whereas a primary theme of the Eastern canon is the search for accommodation in forests. Thus, the mountain hermitage becomes an endlessly valiant image and metaphor in Indian and Chinese poetry, while many characters of British and American literature fight to subdue the sublime forces of the sea in works like *The Tempest*, *The Rime of the Ancient Mariner*, *Lord Jim*, and *Moby-Dick*. Far from embodying a place of refuge, the forests of this continent famously terrified the early white settlers. For the Massachusetts Puritans, the woods were the realm of the devil and devil-worshipping savages. In Nathaniel Hawthorne's short story "Young Goodman Brown," the title character loses his wife, Faith, to the "heathen wilderness," where, during a Black Mass deep in the Massachusetts woods, she is baptized with blood into the service of evil. In the New World, our attitudes toward sea and land were adversarial from the start. We have seldom thought of the natural world as our ally. Even our greatest "nature writers"—Thoreau, John Muir, Edward Abbey— tended to separate city and country into a dichotomous choice between the virtues of the woods and the compromises of civilization. In that view, nature has little to teach us about culture, even about agriculture. And there is probably no other state in this country that embodies our antagonism toward natural landscapes quite like my own. Here in Kentucky, we aren't satisfied just to clear-cut the trees; we then proceed to blow the tops off mountains for pitifully thin seams of coal. Everything else—the stumps, the sandstone, the chemicals, the heavy metals—we dump into the streams below. It's illegal, supposedly, but we do it anyway. I've watched it happen at close range.

Contrast that to what Tagore called the Indian view of reality, with its three phases: *Sat* (the fact that things are), *Chit* (the fact that we know things), and *Ananda* (the love of and union with those things). "For us the highest purpose of this world is not merely living in it, knowing it and making use of it," Tagore writes in his essay "The Religion of the Forest," "but realizing our own selves in it through expansion of sympathy; not alienating ourselves from it and dominating it, but comprehending and uniting it with ourselves in perfect union." That final step seems crucial to me if we are to ever learn anything from the workings of the natural world, if we are ever to shift our role from exploiter to pupil.

One westerner who did manage this paradigm shift was the British economic botanist Sir Albert Howard. The Crown sent him to India in 1903 to teach peasant farmers the benefits of chemical fertilizers and pesticides. But when Howard arrived in Indore, India, he found fertile soils and farms without insect problems. These farmers, he concluded, had already discovered an advisor—the forests that surrounded their fields. For thousands of years, they had watched the trees and microorganisms build topsoil, and they replicated that process in the farming practice that Howard would come to call composting. Quickly, he abandoned his Western mission and concluded, "I could do no better than watch the operations of these peasants and acquire their traditional knowledge as rapidly as possible. For the time being, therefore, I regarded them as my professors of agriculture."

I wonder if Sir Albert Howard and Rabindranath Tagore ever met. They were both middle-aged men at the time of the westerner's assignment, and they certainly would have found in the other a sympathetic foreigner. Howard became the conduit through which India's traditional farming techniques reached the West, where they became known as organic agriculture. He began his first book, *An Agricultural Testament*, by summarizing what he had learned, via peasant farmers, from the forests and fields of India: "Mother earth never attempts to farm without livestock, she always raises mixed crops; great pains are taken to preserve the soil and to prevent erosion; the mixed vegetable and animal wastes are converted into humus; there is no waste; the processes of growth and the processes of decay balance one another; ample provision is made to maintain large reserves of fertility; the greatest care is taken to store the rainfall; both plants and animals are left to protect themselves against disease." Today, organic farmers are still trying to learn, apply, and fine-tune those lessons. And with those lessons, they are trying to combat a dominant industrial agriculture that is driven, from the production of fertilizers to the packaging of food and every step in between, by the intensive use of fossil fuels, compromising antibiotics, fertilizers that create marine dead zones the size of countries, and toxic pesticides that cause ten thousand new cases of cancer a year in humans and kill seventy million birds. It's the opposite of Tagore's notion of sympathy—for the land, for the animals that live on the land, for the often poor people who work on the land. One of Sir Albert Howard's great convictions was that the health of a people could be no better than the health of their land. It seems obvious enough, yet in the United States, our attitude toward the land remains something like that of a Siamese twin who batters and abuses his sibling. That is to say, we seem unwittingly suicidal. It's not necessarily the suicide of a man intent on taking his own life; it's rather the death of an alcoholic who would rather die than quit drinking. And like the alcoholic, when confronted about our behavior by the rest of the world, we make excuses, we become defensive, we lie. We have spiraled down into a solipsism where we can no longer see or understand the *other*—be that other suffering people, other disappearing species, other sick soils, air, and water. Our serotonin is gone, and thus, as studies have shown, so is our empathy. What we sorely need is to find Tagore's idea of *ananda*, an affection for living things outside of the self. We need to look to the natural world to cultivate an East within.

FOR A TIME as a graduate student, I came under the influence of a small offshoot of late modernism known as the concrete poetry movement. These poets set out to spring the word from its narrative context and to treat language as an object, a *visual* medium. Thus, in a concrete poem, words might crash into each other on the page and become new words: *wave* crashes into *rock* and becomes *wrack*, as in waves wracking upon the rocky shore. You get the drift. It was mostly about wordplay and whimsy. At some point, the movement reduced itself to writing one-word poems. For instance, the Scottish poet Ian Hamilton Finlay wrote a one-word poem called "Blueprint." The poem, in its entirety, reads: "wave." You see the joke: the wave is a blue "print" for all of the other blue waves. Eventually, for some of the concrete poets, like Finlay, the word migrated off the page entirely and found a home on gallery walls, in gardens, even floating in ponds. This year, I decided to try my hand at concrete poetry by combining the one-word poem with a piece of ready-made sculpture. I bought a galvanized metal pail and a set of blue stick-on letters at a hardware store. I spelled out the word *METAPHOR* on the side of the pail and hung it from the branch of a young buckeye tree down in the woods. Now, when I take visitors walking in the woods, they invariably pause at the pail, then look at me incredulously. What is it? An old pail hanging from a tree branch, gathering whatever falls? A joke? An oddly placed work of art? A poem? Sometimes I point out that *metaphor* is a Greek word meaning "to carry" or "to transport." But that doesn't clear much up, I suppose. It never seems to satisfy anyone. Is the pail itself the metaphor? And if so, is it a metaphor in the literal, Greek sense, or is it, well, a metaphor of a metaphor? Like the ready-mades that Marcel Duchamp made famous (the men's urinal mounted in a museum, for instance), I think the meaning of my object-poem depends on its displacement: a pail with an odd word on it, hanging from a tree. And like the urinal in a museum, unattached to plumbing, it depends on its uselessness. Such uselessness, by one definition, has *made it* a work of art. What's more, by divesting the pail of its "pail-ness," I'm asking the viewer to consider the very nature of a pail, perhaps for the first time. Perhaps I have elevated the humble pail to the level of poetry. Perhaps the pail is reminding us of the dignity of the ordinary. Perhaps the pail is just saying, "What we owe the world is our attention." We must learn to think with our eyes.

THERE IS A possibly apocryphal story about a young Spanish painter who heard, in 1902, that a boy chasing his dog had stumbled into a cave in Altamira, where he found ancient paintings of wild animals sprawled across the walls. The painter took a train from Barcelona to see the cave for himself. Inside, he found L'Abbé Henri Breuil, a French priest and anthropologist, lying on his back, sketching the magnificent steppe bison, horses, and wild boars that our ancestors had painted thirty-six thousand years earlier, using charcoal, ochre, and hematite. The young painter, whose name was Pablo Picasso, suddenly announced to Breuil, "We have learned nothing!" Which is to say, painting in the West had never again captured that kind of energy, immediacy, authenticity. Picasso would spend the rest of his life dismantling the history of Western art in an effort to find again the power possessed by the cave painters and their subject matter. Thus, he placed a massive bull in the center of his largest painting, *Guernica*, a work memorializing the bombing of a Spanish town by Franco's fascist forces. It's as if the bull were being itself, and *Guernica* a simultaneously modern and prehistoric painting about men betraying the nobility of their own early ancestors through mass slaughter, through barbarously hunting other men for no natural, earthly reason.

A few years ago, archeologists discovered an Indonesian cave painted with eight bipedal figures hunting wild boar and buffalo. These images are at least forty thousand years older than those at Altamira and are thus the oldest pictorial record we have of storytelling in a figurative artwork. What's especially interesting about this cave is that the hunters are depicted as *therianthropes*—humans with animal heads. This helps support the theory that Paleolithic painters were actually shamans, creating these works in a hallucinogenic state of consciousness. A cave is the earth's unconscious. What the shamans painted there they had first seen emerge on the walls inside their own skulls while in trancelike states. A thirty-two-thousand-year-old statuette from western Germany shows a human with a lion's head. One modern San shaman from Namibia spoke of dancing around a fire and seeing a lion inside the flames. The lion consumed the hallucinating shaman and then spit him out—as *a lion*. "I felt the energy of the lion and roared with great authority," recounted the shaman. That must have been what the Upper Paleolithic cave painters felt as well: the charismatic mega-fauna that they depicted gave them a more-than-human power while it restored a connection—drew a *nearness*—to those majestic animals. Today, while humans make up 0.01 percent of all biomass on Earth, we have killed off 83 percent of all wild animals. I do not know of a more heartbreaking statistic—or one that makes me more ashamed of my own species. Unlike our Pleistocene ancestors (who had larger brains than us), we exist in a sad isolation, a self-imposed exile from almost all other life, especially wildlife. We no longer want to become one with the wild animal, a *therianthrope*. We only want to hunt it and hang its head on our walls—a trophy instead of a transformation. This separation from wildness, especially from our own wildness within, has led to arrogance, ignorance, domination, and cruelty. We have become that most unnatural thing—a tamed, sedentary, urban animal, completely disconnected from the basic sources of our biological, psychological, and spiritual health and survival. We don't experience—inhabit—wildness the way our cave-painting ancestors did; we only encounter it perversely via the animals our automobiles kill, or the pandemics caused by our own destruction of the places where wildlife dwells. Picasso, I think, was right. We have not only lost a vital, primal energy within our visual arts, we have lost a vital energy within ourselves. By separating ourselves from the genetic landscapes and animal communities in which we evolved, we have made ourselves small, insular, tame, and narcoleptic. We are turning ourselves into that synthetic dream-animal of Silicon Valley—the technological cyborg. Now, cave art is only so many images on a screen. But once it held the power to transform us, to enliven us, to call us back to our true natures. Those images on the cave walls were an articulation of kinship. The self escaped into an *other*, which was an-other, a larger self. A wholeness.

I HAD AN old drinking buddy who quit drinking. I didn't see him much after that. He got married, had a kid. I took over a baby present and told my friend we should get up. He said he didn't go out much anymore, and I said that was cool, I understood.

Honestly, I haven't seen him since. But in this morning's paper, I read that his kid, his now fifteen-year-old son, was killed last night while walking home. An eighteen-year-old from his high school shot him in the head and left him to die on the side of the road. That shooter's grandfather hid the gun for him. It was stolen, like my friend's son's life.

The next day in Lexington, another teenager shot a classmate dead, and the day after that, the same thing happened again. Twenty years ago, those kids would have settled their beefs with fistfights. But now there are more guns than people in the United States. People with mental illnesses can buy a gun at Walmart, and criminal sociopaths can find their way to a gun show where no background check is required. Or they can just steal the gun. Thirty-thousand Americans kill each other, or themselves, with guns each year. It's all insane, of course, but we've become used to the insanity, inured to the violence. In this country, death is simply the cost of living. However steep, we seem relentlessly willing to pay it.

In Nathaniel Hawthorne's 1844 short story "Rappaccini's Daughter," the narrator, Giovanni Guasconti, moves to the north of Italy to study at the University of Padua. One day, from the balcony of his room, he looks down into a beautiful garden and spies the equally beautiful title character, Beatrice, tending her father's plants. Giovanni is smitten instantly, and Beatrice, for her part, reveals a secret entrance to her father's garden. But a friend of Giovanni's father, Professor Pietro Baglioni, warns the young man away. Rappaccini, he tells Giovanni, is a brilliant but crazed physician who has built his career on the theory that "all medicinal virtues are comprised within those substances which we term vegetable poisons." As a result, his garden functions as a laboratory in which he breeds ever more poisonous plants, plants to which only Beatrice, through constant exposure, has been inoculated. As such, she is always careful never to touch Giovanni when he visits the "Eden of poisonous flowers," even as she falls in love with him. But slowly, Giovanni begins to recognize a sallow, anemic change in his appearance, and he finally becomes distraught when his breath causes a spider in his window to shrivel and die. Rushing down to the garden, Giovanni accuses Beatrice of intentionally trying to trap him in her toxic world. She pleads innocent and says it must be her father's doing. When the triumphant Rappaccini finally appears before Beatrice and Giovanni, his daughter asks, "Wherefore didst thou inflict this miserable doom upon thy child?" Is it misery, Rappaccini replies, "to be as terrible as thou art beautiful?" Beatrice replies, "I would fain have been loved, not feared." Beatrice, in other words, has become an embodiment and a symbol of the United States: in some ways beautiful and alluring but toxic at its core.

What I am talking about is a syndrome of death in this country that reaches far beyond gun violence and mass shootings (though our near-monthly school shootings happen in no other country on Earth). I'm talking about the pesticides and herbicides that kill farmers and consumers alike. I'm talking about the sixty-four thousand Americans who died last year from opioid abuse—double that of a decade ago. I'm talking about the two hundred thousand early deaths each year due to emissions from tailpipes and coal-fired power plants. I'm talking about an infant mortality rate far higher than any European country. I'm talking about the thirty million Americans who drink dangerously contaminated tap water. I'm talking about the 986 Black men killed by police in 2015, 25 percent of whom were unarmed. I'm talking about the 25 percent jump in suicides over the last decade. It's death everywhere you look.

What's remarkable is how blind we are to all of this. Or not exactly blind: more like determined to look away. Our short history has trained us to see through such distorted lenses. We want to believe in the beautiful words of Thomas

Jefferson without thinking too long on the hypocrisy of those words coming from a man who owned six hundred slaves in his lifetime, freeing only seven. We want to take the family to the gleaming confines of Disney World without remembering Andrew Jackson's brutal expulsion of the native Seminoles. For that matter, we want to eat Florida oranges, perfect in appearance, and not worry that they were sprayed with chlorpyrifos, a pesticide that damages children's brains with even minimal exposure.

We suffer from a kind of tragic innocence that must derive from our creation story of cities on hills, benevolent founding fathers, and a divinely sanctioned manifest destiny—in a word, providence. We so badly want to believe the best about ourselves that we simply cannot face how far we have fallen short. So right-wing parents and legislators demand that public schools not teach the facts about slavery or lynching because they don't want their white children to feel bad. Because a republic is all we have ever known, we tend to think of it as unshakable, unimpeachable—which may be why so many of us have abdicated the real work of citizenship. And when we have ceased to be a republic—as has already happened except for one day every four years, and now even that day has become marred by denial and ridiculous voting restrictions—we tend to ignore that reality as well. When asked what kind of government the framers had concocted in Philadelphia in 1787, Benjamin Franklin is famously said to have replied, "A republic, if you can keep it." Well, we haven't kept it. One could draw a pretty simple flowchart to understand why. The arrows would point from powerful corporations—who now enjoy the rights of the First and Fourteenth Amendments to spend money as they please—to the lobbyists they employ and the politicians they buy off. From the corrupted politicians, the chart would flow to a general sense of distrust, disenfranchisement, and apathy on the part of the general public. Another arrow would lead from the corporations to the income inequality—the largest in the developed world—that they helped create: 91 percent of all income increases went to the wealthiest 1 percent from 2009 to 2012. Then, the two arrows pointing from citizen disenfranchisement and income inequality would finally land on guns.

Here's what I mean. For several years, I worked as a janitor at the electric company in my hometown of Louisville, Kentucky. Hundreds of men and women were employed at the coal-fired Mill Power Plant, but the custodial staff weighed in at the bottom of anybody's hierarchy. We made less, we were unskilled, and we performed the most menial work, sweeping up fly ash all day along infernal concrete landings. We were powerless in every way imaginable, and we knew it. And almost all of the men I worked with were gun nuts. One guy, Keith, spent at least half of his biweekly check adding to an arsenal of high-powered handguns and military-style assault rifles. Why? I think because in his mind, guns were the one thing that could substitute for the political and economic power he so clearly lacked. Who had disempowered him? The same corporations that were selling him guns and pills, the same corporations that had usurped his voice as a citizen in a republic, the same corporations that were polluting the air he breathed every day in and around that plant—a plant that was illegally pumping toxins into the Ohio River from which Keith's drinking water came.

The captains of industry who created this climate understood Keith perfectly. If they could keep him distracted with guns—and the threat that liberals might take his guns—they could get back to the business of running the country as they saw fit. They could flood farms with pesticides, flood the market with opioids, flood American waterways with selenium, mercury, and lead. As I said, it's death everywhere you look.

As I mentioned earlier, the philosopher Richard Rorty said that the role of any good government is essentially to reduce suffering and increase sympathy. But in this country, just the opposite happens with astonishing consistency. The federal government uses the cudgel of "deregulation" to unleash all manner of suffering when agencies like the EPA and the Interior Department were created with the fundamental goal of increasing sympathy *through* regulation and enforcement. All of this deregulation is done in the name of small government, which obviously sounds ideologically better than "We want your children ingesting lethal pesticides so the chemical industry will pump more money into our reelection campaigns."

Consider my senator, Mitch McConnell. At the time of my friend's son's death, he had accepted over $1 million from the National Rifle Association. As a result, Kentuckians have about as much chance getting Mitch McConnell to vote for measures that would keep teenagers from getting guns as we have of getting him to vote for mine safety bills or stricter laws against dumping mine waste in our streams and rivers. All of those things are killing Kentuckians, but rather than step to our defense, McConnell actively pushes legislation that makes it easier to kill a classmate, easier to weaken mine safety laws, easier to pollute Kentucky's air and water—you can look it up. Can I blame my friend's son's death solely on McConnell? Of course not. But because of his immense power to control what came up for a vote on the Senate floor when he was majority leader, and because of his unwillingness to allow votes on gun control, he bears much more blame than most. He is Exhibit A that Franklin's republic has gone the way of his lightning rod. And he is proof, if it was ever needed, that our current American version of capitalism and real democracy cannot coexist. In fact, they are mutually exclusive. One is about fairness, solidarity, and protection. The other is about heartless predation in the name of money and power. Supreme Court Justice Louis Brandeis once said, "We may have democracy, or we may have wealth concentrated in the hands of a few, but we can't have both." Today, we clearly have the latter. And that concentrated wealth has put men like McConnell in control of this country and given us this syndrome of death.

Two questions then arise in my mind: How did our country come to manifest such violence? And why do we accept it? A comprehensive answer to either would require two more books, but I'll take a few swings. The fact that this country was built on the enslavement of a foreign people and the genocidal expulsion of a native people will always lay at the core of the first question—all the more so since both are bound together by the ghastly justification of either

Christianizing heathens or destroying them. According to Increase Mather in his account of King Philip's War, it was the God of Providence who helped the Massachusetts Puritans set fire to "hundreds of Wigwams . . . in which men, women and Children (no man knoweth how many hundreds of them) were burnt to death." Almost two hundred years later, in 1853, William Wells Brown, a slave born here in Kentucky, published *Clotel*, this country's first novel by a Black writer. The novel is subtitled *The President's Daughter*, and it hypothesizes miscegenation between Thomas Jefferson and his slave Sally Hemmings well over one hundred years before most presidential historians begrudgingly accepted that fact. In Brown's novel, a circuit rider, based on the real Reverend Thomas Bacon, preaches a sermon to a literally captive audience. He tells the slaves, "Your fathers were poor ignorant and barbarous creatures in Africa, and the whites fitted out ships at great trouble and expense and brought you from that benighted land to Christian America, where you can sit under your own vine and fig tree and no one molest or make you afraid." Shortly before his sermon, the reverend is visited at his plantation by an old friend, Mr. Carlton, who has "drunk too deeply," in the reverend's opinion, from the writings of Rousseau and Thomas Paine. Carlton brings along his nineteen-year-old daughter, Georgiana, who has spent the last five years living in the north. To the reverend's justifications of slavery, his insistence that "the sons of Ham should have the gospel," Georgiana replies over lemonade, "'Thou shalt love thy neighbor as thyself.' This single passage of Scripture should cause us to have respect to the rights of the slave.

True Christian love is of an enlarged, disinterested nature. It loves all who love the Lord Jesus Christ in sincerity, without regard to colour or condition."

What I like about Georgiana's response is that it suggests another root of this country's violence—a relentlessly willful misreading of the religion on which the country was supposedly founded. When a Pharisee asked Jesus what the greatest commandment was, Jesus named the one Georgiana quotes: love of neighbor as self. To her, that alone should have abnegated slavery. It should also go some way to alleviating our great disparity between the rich and poor in this country, to providing better schools for the disadvantaged, to insuring that all Americans have safe drinking water, breathable air, and that they don't live near toxic chemical dumps. It should reject legal discrimination and provide more, not less, asylum for refugees. None of which is happening in this country.

There is a church near my house that puts on a live nativity scene each Christmas. The sign out in front reads DRIVE THRU BETHLEHEM. Those three words say a lot about the contemporary American version of Christianity. It is a Christianity of convenience and a Christianity compatible with an entire economy based on fossil fuels, and therefore an economy that is destroying the very world that Jesus called the kingdom of God. Because the kingdom of God looks nothing like the kingdom of commerce. That was fundamental to Jesus's message. It was a kingdom for outsiders and the destitute. Only they could see the leveling vision he put on offer. Since Jesus's message was meant for Palestinian peasants, it obviously finds an unlikely audience in affluent

America. But the families in the long line of cars seem to ignore all that. Theirs is not a Christianity about finding the kingdom of God "in your midst," as Jesus challenged his generation to do in Luke 11:17. Jesus's vision of the *basileia tou theou*, perhaps better translated as the empire of God, was a radical critique of the Roman Empire, and his crucifixion proved that Rome well understood the potential danger of the critique. But today we ignore all that. The only real reason Christianity took hold in this country is that it promised relief from the fear of death—it promised heaven—through a blood sacrifice of God's son. The only problem with this is that Jesus himself didn't believe this. If Jesus had meant for us to worship him as a god, you think he might have mentioned that during all of his walking and talking around Galilee. He did not. Nowhere in the synoptic Gospels does Jesus call himself the son of God. In fact, when his disciples called him that, he rebuked them. The *entire point* of Christianity is to live *like* Jesus, not to worship him as a Christ. When Jesus told his disciples, "Follow me," he wasn't saying, "Follow me as your redeemer." He was saying, "Follow me as an exemplar of one in which the earthly and the divine have become fused."

But by turning Jesus into a Christ, American Christianity largely ignores the whole social message of the Gospels. It ignores Jesus's charge to return violence with peaceableness. It ignores his admonition to care for the poor and the outcasts, to forgive debts, to avoid the judgment of others. It ignores his urging to be merciful. Instead, we Americans have become the one thing Jesus couldn't abide: hypocrites.

Perhaps nowhere has a moral compass been so lacking

as in our pathological attitude toward the natural world. We seem somehow determined to extract resources from the land in as violent and harmful a way as possible. We destroy the Appalachian Mountains for the coal that lies within them, then when the coal is nearly gone, we replace it, not with wind and solar power but with hydraulic fracking that leaches gas into groundwater. Rather than invest in electric cars powered by solar-charged lithium-ion batteries, we continue to build offshore oil rigs as if we have learned nothing from the BP *Deepwater Horizon* disaster. How to understand this pathology? It is inescapably a patriarchal form of violence (in all of my years trespassing on Kentucky strip mines, I never once saw a woman detonating explosives; and anyone who actively opposes the coal industry risks physical, masculine intimidation and abuse).* Up through the Neolithic era, goddesses were revered throughout Mesopotamia, and all of their earthly groves were sacred—and treated as such. There was no history, only cycles: seasonal, migrational, menstrual. But the Bronze Age brought the patriarchal violence of Gilgamesh, who killed the horned bull of the goddess Ishtar. Gilgamesh was soon followed by a Judeo-Christian sky god who demanded that pagan forest groves be destroyed and that his people turn their gaze toward his ineffable, heavenly presence. His people created a new, linear narrative that begins in Eden and ends in heaven. The migration—along with the eventual

---

* West Virginia strip miners threatening July 4th picnickers on Kayford Mountain: https://www.youtube.com/results?search_query=larry+gibson +miners.

migration from Judaism to Christianity—became upward, one-directional, a pilgrim's progress. That sense of moral progress eventually transmogrified into a belief in technological progress. Both will eventually lead us to a utopia of ease and abundance—whether here on the earth or in the hereafter—no matter the ecological or moral costs. This worldview upended the pagan, Greco-Roman idea of cyclical time and sacred groves. The Christianized West brought a violence to the natural world that had never been seen before. Certainly Eastern and Indigenous cultures had never seen anything like it. Perhaps going back to the invention of the plow in the seventh century, we cannot shake the belief that the natural world must be attacked, ripped open, degraded to make it yield our sustenance. As a result, we tend to see the natural world as an adversary, something altogether foreign and separate from us. Indeed, we have spent so much time trying to separate ourselves from the natural world, we no longer really see it as anything other than peripheral scenery, a space to be traversed on our way to an air-conditioned building or automobile. We even talk blithely about abandoning this toxic world for life on Mars. And in a way it makes sense. So many Americans have traded the actual world for a virtual one, they would hardly notice the change in environment. Our collective lives are becoming one long withdrawal from the natural world—a world that is now, like the goddess Ishtar, taking its revenge all around us. It's death everywhere you look.

MY RESPONSE TO the election of Donald J. Trump as president of the United States was as much a surprise to me as it was to my friends. I became a land artist. Of sorts. The abandoned strip mines of Eastern Kentucky became my canvas, and trees became my medium. If Trump was going to renounce the Paris Climate Accord and try to repeal every piece of environmental regulation President Obama had set in place, I could at least get to work planting hardwood trees, knowing each would sequester twenty-two tons of carbon in its lifetime (worldwide, forests capture 24 percent of all carbon emissions). Better yet, I could recruit friends to help me plant. We could call ourselves Kentucky Writers and Artists for Reforestation.

So we did. On the first Earth Day after the election, in a freezing rain, about forty of us drove up to a strip mine on the Cumberland Plateau and we planted 2,500 seedlings from dozens of native species, the species that were standing there before the bulldozers arrived and scraped that mountain bare. But did this make me a land artist? In my mind, it did not. We were a bunch of creative types planting trees, which was undeniably a good thing. But it wasn't art. Not yet.

Any traditional definition of art involves a frame, some kind of confined space. Art, as we usually understand it, takes place in a book or a gallery or a theater. But I first began thinking about the limitations of such spaces when I came across the work of a small group of American land artists, men (they were all men) like Robert Morris, Robert Smithson, and Walter De Maria, who in the late sixties started digging their own rows in the American West with massive backhoes. There was nothing particularly "environmental" about the early land artists, as they came to be called, or their earthworks. In fact, much of the early land art consisted of gashes cut into the desert. "Instead of a paintbrush to make his art," wrote Robert Smithson, "Robert Morris would like to use a bulldozer."

Land art, or earth art, was a response—like everything else in the sixties—to the establishment. Land artists were unhappy with the gallery economy that turned art into just another commodity to festoon the walls of the rich, not that this was anything new. Nevertheless, the earth artists aimed to take their work beyond the "white cube" of the gallery and to situate it in a landscape where the art could not be commodified because the landscape *was* the art. They were good Marxists even if they weren't great ecologists.

In 1970, the same year as the first Earth Day, the Canadian government halted Smithson's *Island of Broken Glass* over fears that its two tons of glass shards dropped on a rock outcropping would harm nesting seabirds and seals. It's hard to imagine today that this never occurred to Smithson himself, who would become famous for creating the United States' most recognized earthwork, *Spiral Jetty*, a swirling path of basalt that extends out into Utah's Great Salt Lake like some huge pre-Cambrian organism. But, perhaps stung by the criticism, Smithson began writing letters to mine operators in Ohio, offering to reclaim strip mine sites in an effort to create what his wife and fellow land artist Nancy Holt called "a functional or necessary aesthetics, not art cut off from society, but rather an integral part of it." Holt herself took over the project when Smithson died in a plane crash a year later at age thirty-five.

Holt's idea of an art integral to society became a point

of departure from the undeniably masculine violence of the early land art, toward a new earth art that took on ecological dimensions and an environmental ethos. Put another way, she was calling for a marriage of *aesthetics* and *activism*.

That's what I wanted to achieve with our reforestation efforts. We had already done the activist part—planting trees on strip mines—and now we needed to somehow elevate that to the level of art. To do that, I felt we needed to incorporate three intermingling genres often associated with earthworks: conceptual art, performance art, and sculpture.

The conceptual element came first, when I realized 2017 was the eight-hundredth anniversary of the Magna Carta's Charter of the Forest. In 1217, King Henry III sealed the *Carta Foresta* as a companion to the more famous document. It established the rights of free men to gather essential resources from the king's royal forest without the punitive threat of amputation or even death, as had existed since William the Conqueror. In essence, the Charter of the Forest allowed commoners to hunt, pasture, and collect fuel for cooking and heating in the royal forests. As such, the Charter of the Forest is generally considered the English-speaking world's first environmental law, the first legal document to recognize the natural realm as a commons and to guarantee rights and privileges to those outside the aristocracy—commoners. What's more, it set the groundwork for establishing public lands and ensuring their access and protection as a basic human right. America's national parks celebrated their hundredth anniversary in 2016, but their legal origins began seven hundred years earlier.

So my concept was this: we would find a former strip mine that had been converted into public land and plant eight hundred acorns to celebrate the Charter of the Forest's octocentennial. I called up a colleague at the University of Kentucky, Chris Barton. He had started an incredibly successful reforestation initiative called Green Forests Work a few years back. It was the summer of 2017 when I contacted him, and I knew we couldn't plant saplings in the fall; they wouldn't get enough rain to survive. But I thought if we planted acorns, they could lie dormant over the winter and wait for spring precipitation. I explained that I was thinking of this venture as an "art installation" to be called *800 Acorns*. (Beginning in 1982, the German artist Joseph Beuys began installing *7,000 Oaks* around Kassel, Germany, as part of Documenta 7, and my project would clearly be a descendant—literally, acorns—of that.) I asked Chris if he thought it was nuts. He said he didn't and that his organization had some money it could put toward my project. This was one of two lessons that I was quickly learning about being a land artist: get someone else to pay for your crazy idea. What's more, Chris found a ten-acre site that indeed had been a strip mine before it was converted a few years back into part of the Daniel Boone National Forest.

So I had the conceptual piece in place. As for the sculptural, I know I just wrote dismissively about using bulldozers to create land art, but that's exactly how *800 Acorns* began. Because the soil and rock of an abandoned strip mine has become so compacted by heavy machinery, it would be impossible to plant anything there other than an exotic weed called lezpedeza (which is what coal companies usually plant in the name of "reclamation"). Consequently, before we could start sowing acorns, local bulldozer operators had to come in with huge taildraggers and essentially rip two half-mile troughs into the compacted ground. It was in that loosened rock and soil that we would plant.

My idea was to create a colonnade of oaks: four hundred on each side of what would become a walking path. As the oaks grew, their crowns would slowly grow sculpturally, architecturally together into something resembling (at least in my imagination) the nave of a forest cathedral. They would echo the ancient correspondences between forests and the temples of the gods, between trees and columns. I thought of Baudelaire's poem "Correspondences," which begins: "Nature is a temple where living pillars / Sometimes let out confusing words."

I spoke my own possibly confusing words about the future cathedral forest to about fifty writers, artists, students, and teachers who gathered one Saturday morning in October to help me plant acorns. And that is the second lesson I learned about land art: delegate work to others, then take credit for the results (did Robert Smithson place a single rock on *Spiral Jetty*?). The day was sunny and warm. Chris gave a quick demonstration of how to plunge a dibble stick (a kind of spade) into the ground to create a *V* in which to drop the acorn, before replacing the soil. Next, we had to use a bamboo rod to stake a net tube over the hole to fend off squirrels—that was crucial. After this tutorial, my friend and Irish scholar Jonathan Allison read from W. H. Auden's poem, "Bucolics," which ends, "A culture is no better than its woods."

Then we all set off in pairs, as if departing the ark to re-plenish a barren world. We staggered the acorns ten feet apart on each side of the trail. The planting was leisurely, and there was much conversation, none of which, I was pleased to notice, involved Donald J. Trump. Some partic-ipants brought their young children to drop acorns in the ground. Gradually, the foot-high pink net tubes began to punctuate the path, and it occurred to me that for now, we were inadvertently applying a sort of Christo-treatment to this rolling landscape. The tubes looked unnatural and re-petitive as with a Christo installation. Yet they were also oddly, aesthetically pleasing. And after all, they were bio-degradable and would soon be displaced when saplings knocked them out of the way. Christo too has gotten a lot of volunteer help over the years.

That was the performance element of *800 Acorns*. If sculpture—future trees—was the aesthetic aspect, then planting them was at once the activist and "theatrical" aspect, to use art critic Michael Fried's term. He meant it as a pejorative, in that performance somehow debases the static contemplation of a piece of sculpture. But because the scale of earthworks is often so vast, one must often participate *in* the sculpture itself. Around the same time land art was emerging as a genre, Joseph Beuys put forward an idea he called "social sculpture," in which "everyone is an artist." That, I like to think, is what our crew was that day: a collective of artists who embodied and created a work of both aesthetic and social sculpture.

What's more, according to another critic, Lucy R. Lippard, the fact that our performance was so repetitive—digging, planting, digging, planting—would suggest to her that it was also a kind of religious ritual, like Trappist monks chanting eight times a day or Buddhist monks bowing over and over as they make their pilgrimage to a sacred shrine. "Of those who have tried to replace society's passive expectations of art with a more active model," Lippard wrote in 1963, "many have chosen to call their activities 'rituals.'" Certainly, the planting of trees has to be one of the most ancient rituals, right up there with stacking and arranging rocks. The purpose of ritual, I suppose, is to dramatize some system of values. The repetition of that ritual reminds participants of what those values are. It also enacts those values over and over, whether through bowing, chanting, or dropping acorns into a hole. I suspect the fifty of us planting trees that October had a diverse set of values and reasons for our ritual: some spiritual, some political, some ecological, some parental. But as we worked, I began to sense that our cumulative repetition, our act of social sculpture, had also produced a certain kind of alchemy. We started to see this space as something other than an abandoned strip mine. In his classic work *The Sacred and the Profane*, Mircea Eliade wrote, "Where the sacred manifests itself in space, *the real unveils itself*, the world comes into existence." This, to me, is the crucial connection between art, ritual, and the sacred (however we interpret that term). The enactment of, or the idea of, the sacred does not change the world in any way; it simply *reveals* the world for what it is, for what we have been unable to see. It removes our blinders. The oak trees that grow here will be no different from any of the other oaks in this watershed. But the ritual of planting them, and the ritualistic space they will create—a colonnade that frames a clearing, a path—will, I hope, call visitors more intensely into the presence of the natural world. Art will be the threshold back into the real.

As we planted, a team of graduate students from the UK School of Design (see second lesson of land art) began to place posts in the ground, staggered at eighth-mile intervals among the acorns. These posts would display pastoral poems laser-etched into handsome oak plaques. My idea was that future visitors to this site could wander down the right side of the path, reading and ruminating on the poems as they walked, then return back on the opposite side, taking in those oak-shaded bucolics. The first poem the grad students mounted was W. S. Merwin's "Place." It begins, "On the last day of the world / I would want to plant a tree." To plant that tree is an act of defiance, not forethought. It is a way of saying, I still believe in the laws of nature, not the laws of the market, which made this the last day. Merwin himself was an inspiration for *800 Acorns* since he spent the last forty years of his life planting palm trees—over three thousand—on a deracinated hillside at his home on Maui. After the students finished placing the plaque, I read it again alongside the poet Maurice Manning.

"Can you imagine how pleased Merwin would be," Maurice finally said, "to see his poem standing here, in this setting?" I said I hoped he would, because I hadn't actually asked his permission. Maurice grinned. "It's just amazing," he went on, "to think about all the people who will get to read this poem in this way, in this place." I also hoped that the poem would draw the landscape closer to them, draw it into greater focus. I wanted all the poems to stand in conversation with the trees for as long as either stood, and I wanted the people who visited this site to join that conversation, even if—especially if—it was held in silence.

But Maurice was right. Unlike traditional sculpture housed in museums, time does play an elemental role in land art—in the sense that the elements will bring change to it. The sculpture we created is a living thing, and it will face all the travails of life in the open air. It will grow, die, and eventually, if *Homo sapiens* stays out of the way, be replaced by another successional forest. The poems will in time become illegible, and their posts will rot. But by then the trees will have absorbed almost eighteen thousand tons of carbon. They will provide sanctuary for the region's 250 species of songbirds, two-thirds of which are in decline because of habitat loss like the strip mining that once ravaged this particular place. They will prevent mudslides and flooding, and they will purify local drinking water. And when they finally die and decompose, fungi, termites, and beetle larvae will turn them into the soil that will start the cycle all over again.

When we reached the end of both rows and all the acorns were in the ground, our collective hoisted dibble sticks over our shoulders, and we began a slow march back in the direction we came. There, where we had begun our planting, architect Bruce Swetnam and a crew of UK graduate students were finishing construction of what would become at once a small meditation hut and a passageway into *800 Acorns*. When I pitched Bruce the idea of possibly helping build a modest kiosk to mark and explain the site, he and his grad students saw a much more compelling opportunity. They first built a model so I could understand their vision, then raised the money to bring it to scale (see both lessons one and two of being a land artist). Their idea for the back wall was to build a thick wire cage filled with blocks of coal to remind visitors what had been extracted here at one time. In a sense, Bruce and his students were bringing a "dirty secret" to light, bringing the ugly history of this site up to the surface. I loved that. A small wooden bench seemed to float in front of the coal cage, and a cedar wall stood at an angle across from it.

The entrance into this hut is much narrower than the opposite side that faces our planting site. The entrance suggests a threshold into something mysterious, like the entrance into a forest. Then the walls of the hut open up, releasing visitors onto the path of *800 Acorns*. In this sense, the hut is, to my mind, a profoundly liminal structure, marking the transition from the gravel road below into a poetic space that has been made so by both the ritual of its creation and the sculptural presence of the oaks.

But before visitors pass through this prism of a building, they can pause on the bench and read, etched into the cedar wall, Wendell Berry's poem "Planting Trees." It describes the poet carrying in a bucket twenty saplings he would plant where others—"the ancient host"—had fallen or been cut. "I return to the ground its original music," Berry writes, just as we had done that day. He imagines this small stand growing first above the grass, then the weeds, then the "horizon of men's heads." "I have made myself a dream to dream / of its rising, that has gentled my nights," Berry writes, then he imagines them rising still "when I / no longer rise in the mornings."

As we all gathered around the meditation hut, Maurice Manning told the students, "What you did here today in a few hours will last for three hundred years. Think about that." They actually did seem to be cogitating on the image of towering trees far outliving them, yet still manifesting for centuries the ecological benefits of the students' labor. Then, after explaining to the younger planters the singular importance of Wendell Berry's writing over the last sixty years, Maurice read "Planting Trees" aloud. I thought of one of Berry's titles, *A Timbered Choir*, and I thought again about Joseph Beuys's idea of social sculpture. That notion, it seems to me, doesn't apply only to humans. The trees that eventually rise here will themselves be a work of social sculpture. In recent years, scientists have discovered that trees of the same species growing together use their root systems to communicate with one another and exchange nutrients when certain members of the timbered choir are in need. That, I realized, is what Beuys's *7,000 Oaks* project was ultimately about: trying to place human beings back into a symbiotic connection with the nonhuman world—specifically, the arboreal world. It was *trees*, after all, that guided the evolution of our prehensile limbs and binocular vision. They made us who we are. To drop eight hundred acorns in eight hundred holes seems like a small act of propitiation for helping to ensure our survival over the last two hundred thousand years.

As we slowly dispersed that October day, a young activist stopped and said to me, "You know, you get tired of always being against everything. Sometimes you just want to be *for* something. That's what we did here today."

I agreed. My work was done.

THE FIRST AND second weeks of November are the best time to do some of the worst work around here: trying, ultimately with Sisyphean futility, to eradicate an invasive species called bush honeysuckle. This shrub arrived in the US from Asia in 1897 as an ornamental plant, but it quickly escaped its garden confines to flourish in eastern forests. It leafs out earlier and retains its leaves longer than almost any other tree or shrub. It also doesn't mind low sun exposure, and its roots produce a chemical that inhibits the root growth of other species. As a result, indigenous trees and shrubs have a difficult time competing for space and light. The advantage of native plants in any landscape is that thousands of other living species have coevolved with them and depend on them. The best providers of nutrients in most eastern US forests are the "keystone" species of oaks, hickories, cherries, pines, and maples—the very trees that luckily dominate our property. A single oak can support over five hundred species of caterpillars, crucial to native birds, while an Asian ginkgo tree hosts only five species. That's crucial when over 430 bird species in North America are now at risk of extinction. What's more, exotic plants provide birds and insects with almost no nutritional value. Birds do eat honeysuckle berries, but that only serves to further spread this noxious weed. What is most obvious on our western slope is that the honeysuckle is crowding out many other trees and thus steadily decreasing diversity. So, because I don't want to live in a monoculture, I spend some long, exhausting days in November, trying to kill honeysuckle. This is the best time of year for this work because, since only honeysuckle still clings to its leaves, the bush is easy to spot.

Today is sunny and mild for November, so I grab my chainsaw and pruning shears, then head down into the woods. I tramp over the mossy outcrops and balance my gear precariously at the edge of the cliff tops, where most of the remaining honeysuckle grows. All the noise chases away a large buck, who jumps an ancient, crumbling stone wall at the edge of our property. If the honeysuckle is a foot high, I simply pull it up at its roots. If it's over two feet, I clip it to the ground. If it's a mature, ten-foot tree, I reach for the chainsaw. Then I apply an herbicide to the remaining stump. If I don't, next year's growth around that stump will be even worse. A purist will tell you I should be digging out all the stumps and avoiding the chemicals. But that would consume so much time, the honeysuckle would be spreading faster than I could stop it. And I would probably have a heart attack in the process.

When I first moved to Nonesuch, I grandly informed one of my neighbors I was going to make it a year's work to clear all the honeysuckle from my property. She replied, "You better make it a life's work." Since then, I've come to understand what she meant. Despite my diligence, birds still spread honeysuckle seed—a mature shrub holds about a million seeds—and I still return to the onerous annual task. Why do I bother with it? I ask myself every year. The only answer is that I want to leave this land better than I found it. I don't mean that I want to leave it *to* somebody; I simply want to leave the land to itself. I want to improve this land, not because I own it, but because I want to belong to it.

Let me explain what I mean by way of a short poem from the criminally neglected Lorine Niedecker:

> Black Hawk held: In reason
> land cannot be sold,
> only things to be carried away,
> and I am old.

> Young Lincoln's general moved,
> pawpaw in bloom,
> and to this day, Black Hawk,
> reason has small room.

Black Hawk was a Sauk war chief who defended the tribe's original territory in Illinois as Andrew Jackson sought to push all Indigenous peoples west of the Mississippi River. Black Hawk fought against, among other soldiers, Abraham Lincoln, in the Black Hawk War of 1832. In Niedecker's poem, we hear Black Hawk making the case that only man-made things can reasonably be sold. Land cannot. But the Sauk leader lost what would turn out to be the final Indian war, and Niedecker, who lived her whole life on Black Hawk Island, Wisconsin, addresses the old chief's ghost: hundreds of years later, we still do not listen to reason.

I myself am on the side of Black Hawk and Niedecker. One of my bedrock political convictions, however utopian it may sound, is that a person should not be allowed to own what that person, or another person, did not make. This includes water, coal, oil, gas, the airwaves, plant DNA—and land. I am convinced that every social ill in this country (and the world) originated when one group of people— usually white—commanded for itself something it had no right to because, by natural right, it belongs to everyone. Put another way, epidemiologists Richard Wilkinson and Kate Pickett have shown that the societal problems of this county—infant mortality, violence, incarceration, substance abuse—derive from income inequality (the worst in the developed world). Quite obviously, income inequality is the result of a small group of powerful people taking as their own something that never belonged to them in the first place. And the very first thing they took was land.

What would I suggest instead? As I wrote back on my boat, when I was trying to sketch out a watershed economy, all of the things I just mentioned as *given*, not manmade, should be controlled collectively by each individual watershed. Right now in the adjacent city of Lexington, water rates are high and problems constant because the water company is controlled by a foreign corporation with a terrible environmental record. But there should, "in reason," as Black Hawk would have it, be no private water companies or coal companies or oil companies. Just examine the environmental records of each and you'll understand why. But beyond even that, all of that natural wealth should rightly be shared in common by everyone in the watershed.

But what about my original concern, the land? I would personally like to convince my eight neighbors to join me in putting all of our property—about one hundred acres—into a land trust. What that means is we would separate the value of our homes from the value of the land. We would form a nonprofit organization that would hold the land as a trust, in perpetuity. The land would belong to no one; it would belong to itself. When or if a family moved or died, only its house and the improvements the family made to the house would be estimated in the sales price. Improvements made to the land, such as planting shade trees or cutting bush honeysuckle, could also be figured into the sales price. But the value of the land would remain the same. No one could make a profit on something other than their own labor. If everyone did this, housing would become more affordable. Speculation would end.

Of course, that's never going to happen. I would more likely convince my neighbors to join a doomsday cult and sit on their roofs every night, waiting for the heavens to open. So I'll just sweat it out down here on my own, trying to make this hillside more habitable to the native trees and their native residents and pollinators. I'll recite Niedecker's poem over and over as an incantation, until I've summoned for company the ghost of Black Hawk himself.

LAST SUMMER I discovered that one can make a pretty respectable screech owl house out of an eight-foot-by-ten-inch plank of cedar. The result is a house about the size of a large shoebox with a three-inch round opening and a roof fastened by a door hinge to allow for cleaning. With a skill saw, a jigsaw, and rudimentary carpentry skills, I cobbled together three boxes and hung them about fifteen feet up in some of the larger trees around the house. Tonight at dusk, and every night for the last few weeks, I've watched a small gray head poking through the hole of a box nailed to a walnut tree thirty feet from our back deck. The screech owl's dark ears stand erect above its large, yellow eyes. It's still apparently too early in winter for this male to begin courtship rituals, which include a monotonic trill that signals to the female he has found a suitable cavity in which to raise their annual clutch of owlets. When the female does appear, the male will get busy, fetching her the carcasses of juncos and other small birds to prove his worth as a provider for her future brood. Then, late after dark, I will hear his tremulous, plaintive whinny, which is one of the best and strangest sounds in the Kentucky night. What does it mean? Surely not what I think it means. The owl speaks owl and I speak human. He surely has no use for the word *plaintive*. But still I listen. I don't need to know his meaning to take pleasure in his distant company. And I repay that pleasure with a wooden box nailed to a tree. He has no idea why I hung it there, why I want to sit out in the cold with my binoculars for half an hour and watch him watch the world.

But for now, everything seems absolutely still in this screech owl's world. He rotates his head slightly to scan the clearing surrounding his tree. Then, after about a half hour of this perusing, he lays back his ears and suddenly launches his small gray body from the hole. He loses altitude quickly before leveling off just inches above the ground to disappear into the low forest understory. And as he vanishes, this is what I think: unlike the large-brained, self-conscious *Homo sapiens*, the owl never doubts itself. The owl knows exactly what it is about. The owl is about the night, the mice, the hunger to be ever only itself. As the old mountaineers of Eastern Kentucky might have said: take a lesson from it.

WHILE HAVING DINNER with a friend and her new, rather conservative husband, I was mounting one of my usual critiques of the United States when the new husband said, "Well, if you don't like America, where would you rather live?" I rattled off about fifteen countries in quick succession. It turned out to be a short dinner.

When James Baldwin heard a similar question about why he didn't just "go back to Africa," the Harlem native replied, "The Negro has been formed by this nation, for better or for worse, and does not belong to any other." Like Baldwin, I did not choose to be born an American—nor would I have, given the opportunity. I wish I hadn't been born into a corrupt plutocracy, a place where our political representatives are, for the most part, self-serving extortionists. I wish I hadn't been born into a country of intractable prejudice and staggering inequality. Given a choice, I would have entered the world a Scandinavian, like my forebears. I would have chosen a country where politics is a transparent exchange of ideas, not money, and where citizens enjoy the highest standards of living in the world. I would have chosen a country that has largely solved the problems of the nation-state through a cooperative contract called democratic socialism. But I wasn't born in Norway; I was born in Petersburg, Virginia—the heart of the Confederacy. And I am no more likely to move to Norway than Baldwin was likely to move to Liberia. He didn't choose America; America chose him. And he was going to have to live with that, in America, whether he liked it—whether white Americans liked it—or not.

Since I too was born here, since this is my home, I must live with and grapple with the problems of this country. I must take responsibility for where and when I do live. I have no flag to wave, no abstract notion of nationality to defend. I *would* defend the watershed where I live against predatory industrialists, as I have done in the past. And I have no problem spiking trees to defend them from clear-cuts, or pouring sugar and sand into the oil ducts of a Caterpillar bulldozer—if it came to that. Though I don't think industrial sabotage is a particularly effective way to draw attention to one's political cause, I do retain that possibility as a viable option if natural places and crucial wildlife habitats are under imminent industrial threat.

Of the 195 countries in the world, only a handful display on their national flags a living thing, and often that thing is a war eagle. (I prefer Lebanon's flag, with its green cedar tree standing against a red and white background, supposedly a symbol of peace.) The state flag of Kentucky is particularly ridiculous: two white men shaking hands, one in a suit and one in cartoonish leather stockings. No sign anywhere of the Shawnee, the Cherokee, the Chickasaw, or the Osage. No sign of James Baldwin's ancestors. "United We Stand" reads the Kentucky flag. United *who* stands? For and against whom? The American flag isn't much better—an exercise in busyness. What's more, its fifty jumbled stars indicate a nation far too large to truly inspire loyalty, unity, or incorruptibility. A couple of years ago, when the University of Kentucky men's basketball team—all Black young men—took a knee during the playing of the national anthem, a white Kentucky legislator introduced a bill to ban kneeling during the anthem in our great commonwealth. One wonders what experience he has ever had with police brutality or discrimination in housing, employment, daily life. But more importantly, we should take this imbecile's bill as a warning to be on guard against any political state that *demands* our compulsory allegiance—especially a nation like ours, built on legally, arbitrarily sanctioned violence against its own citizens.

In 2020, in my hometown of Louisville, armed plainclothes police broke into an apartment unannounced and then were surprised when the Black man who lived there tried to defend himself with his own licensed gun. So they shot to death his unarmed girlfriend, Breonna Taylor. There were no drugs on the premises, and Taylor had never been convicted of a crime—nor had her boyfriend, Kenneth

Walker. So the police invented lies to justify their own in-
eptitude. Every Black man and woman in the West End of
Louisville knows "liberty and justice for all" is nothing more
than a vacuous sentiment written by white people for white
people. I myself do not know what it feels like to be a Black
man or woman in this country, but I know enough to understand why they do not want to pledge allegiance to the flag
for which that kind of brutality stands. I don't want to either.
Like the Stoics *cosmopolitans*, I am (at least in my mind) a
citizen of the cosmos, of the planet, of my own Kentucky
watershed. I would happily renounce my US citizenship, and
have investigated doing so, except that such a renunciation
requires an "exit fee" that runs into the thousands of dollars, and there unfortunately exists no passport for being a
global citizen. So here I stand symbolically, a citizen of the
microcosm and the macrocosm. If there were a flag depicting
the Milky Way, I would salute that. If there were a flag depicting the beautiful "blue marble" that is the planet Earth,
I would salute that. If the Inner Bluegrass of Kentucky made
a flag woven from bluestem and buffalo clover, I would happily salute that—even pledge my allegiance.

THOUGH I DISAGREED with biologist Jerry Coyne earlier in
this journal about the hypothetical thoughts of a hypothetical creator, I can certainly get behind his statement, "Evolution tell us where we came from, not where we can go." In
that sense, the imagination remains a liberating evolutionary force, one that can shape the future until it gets sabo-
taged by its lack of imagination—by fear, hatred, rapaciousness. *Homo sapiens* resolutely does *not*, as the Stoics

urged, "live according to nature." At every turn, we try to dominate, manipulate, and transcend nature through our technology and our moral blindness. We have turned the evolutionary gift of rationality into a suicidal instrument of self-harm, perhaps self-annihilation. Our rapacity will be our undoing. Or as Emerson said, "The end of the human race will be that it will eventually die of civilization."

THE WINTER-DESPERATE DEER have finally ripped apart the hedge apples that lay scattered in our neighbor's field like a hundred green corpus callosum. The medusa-headed tree itself, also called an Osage orange, now reveals its spooky bare branches in this heatless January light. An old field guide of mine says about this pliant wood: "Indians made bows out of it. And we make police clubs." A few summers back, an off-duty cop named Daniel Pantaleo used such a club to strangle a defenseless Black man, Eric Garner, for selling cigarettes outside a strip mall on Staten Island. The cell phone video is unmistakable. Now Eric Garner is dead, and the cop who killed him is drinking with his buddies in some Bay Street dive. How in this country can something so elemental as a tree speak such different meanings to Eric Garner and Erik Reece? One sees firewood for the winter, one felt the surrounding ghosts of a lynch mob. One sees carbon converted into oxygen. One felt a police baton choking off his final breath.

EARLY THIS MORNING, I wake to the beautiful confluence of a full moon refracting the sun's light out over a blanket of snow, a glowing white world. Yesterday, we had a storm that encased every tree branch, every blade of grass in a sheathing of ice. It was a landscape completely drained of color except for a single cardinal that moved like a pulsing red light outside our window. Then the snow followed, replacing the clattering ice with complete stillness and quiet. So I build a fire in the woodstove, pull on my muck boots, and grab my walking stick that leans beside the front door. I consider for a moment this well-purposed companion I made fifteen years earlier after another ice storm. I cut its shaft from a toppled apple tree and the handle from the forked branch of a fallen pear tree. Apple and pear met at a mortised joint a foot below the stick's thumb notch. In some utopian mythologies, the pear represents the apple's redemption from its tragic role in the Judeo-Christian creation story. If the apple is a symbol of humankind's fall, then the pear predicts its rise back into union with the natural world and all humankind. And if I'm remembering correctly, the triangular pear even stands for liberty, fraternity, and equality. That French triad is certainly as alien in this country today as an apple tree grafted onto a pear. But my utopian emblem will serve me well as I try to navigate the western slope and the narrow trails above the creek.

The bird feeders are all spinning with the presence of house finches, nuthatches, and chickadees on every perch. The stone Buddha that sits imperturbably beneath them wears on its head a conical, comical fez made of snow. Two finches sit on its shoulders, waiting for their turn at the safflower seed. The snowfall has turned the woods into a white page written only in the alphabet of trees: the spindly locusts, the hoary sycamores, the regal spruce, the imperious elms and walnuts. The young cedars bow low like green hermits huddled in silent prayer. The tall trees cast clean-lined shadows that seem so much more intense falling across a deep, drifting snow. No humans or dogs have ventured out this morning, so the white field of shadows still possesses an untrammeled gracefulness. Even the ground-loving, dark-eyed junco now clings to the thistle feeder or the forsythia. With snow erasing the understory of plants, leaves, and grasses, the trees articulate themselves more boldly and elegantly. It is in such austere verticality that they don't seem to need us, the animals of the understory, the creatures who do not wholly—or who have forgotten how to—worship the sun.

Beyond the feeders, three bluebirds perch on the dead branch of a walnut tree, while two downy woodpeckers call to each other in the higher branches that glisten with ice against the blue sky. A small group of young deer move timidly along a narrow ledge down below, while a single winter wren flits around their hooves. My own feet crunch a new path down into the woods, and the hardened ice under the snow makes the walking easier. When I reach the flat bottom, I move beneath the limestone rock face now covered in dense layers of long icicles. Were I walking *beneath* the ground here, I might observe calcium carbonate slowly dissolving this limestone into stalactites that bear a remarkable resemblance to these spears of ice. The process seems to be the same here above ground ("stalactite" comes from the Greek word meaning "dripping"), except that changing weather—unknown in a cave—is creating these icicles at a speed unfathomable to their subterranean kin. In one place, where the limestone juts out from the rim rock, the ice almost forms a translucent curtain that seems drawn to obscure some clandestine encounter, between a pair of raccoons perhaps. As I move closer to the base of the cliff, I see a rosette of saxifrage leaves extending from the frozen moss and already framing the balled, emerging head that will eventually become its airy white flowers.

Further on, I loop back around the two ancient sycamores and follow the creek upstream. The aging cedars now wear only the thinnest gauze of bark. The only sounds I hear are the creek moving in one direction, and above it, the birds moving in another, like two rivers flowing along opposite paths. High in the canopy, a blue jay imitates the cry of the hawk soaring above it; I don't know why. After a snowfall, the water runs as clear as it ever does. And the air feels just as clear and pure. I am never so aware of my breathing as when the air entering and exiting my lungs is this cold. I don't have to be told by some Zen master to count my breaths; my breaths seem to be counting themselves as they labor in and out. And what they say is always the same: *This is the life, the only life, and you are in it, right now, moment to moment.* The flowing creek, it seems to me, takes a perfect measure of such moments.

I READ IN the *New York Times* today that after an acrimonious divorce, billionaire Harry Macklowe and his former wife, Linda, have sold off their modern art collection for $922 million. A Rothko went for $82 million, a Giacometti for $78 million, a Warhol for $18 million. And so on. It got me thinking about the art Melissa and I have collected together over the years. Ernest Hemingway once complained to Gertrude Stein that he couldn't afford the art he really wanted to buy: Picasso, Gris, Braque. As with most things regarding Hemingway, I have reached exactly the opposite opinion. I can afford (though often not easily) at least some of the art I want to hang in my house because most of that art was created by local painters and photographers. We hear much talk these days about "buying local," but it seems to me that very little of that talk ever gets extended to art. But what I've found, and certainly Central Kentucky is not unique in this way, is that there exists, all around us, amazing local art to see and to procure. Along with talking to local farmers and buying their crops, I also like to talk to local artists and support their work. It began very modestly with a Northern Kentucky artist named Randall Plowman. Every day, he made a four-by-four-inch original collage and sold it online for $25. I bought a few and so did Melissa, before we were married (now they all line up along our mantel, behind the woodstove). Then one Christmas, Melissa bought me a large canvas by Lennon Michalski, called *Milkweed*. It looks a bit like a cross between Cy Twombly and Paul Klee, yet remains wholly original. We had seen the painting at a local group show, and I'd talked about how much I admired Lennon's work. Melissa went back to his studio and said I loved the piece, but she wasn't sure she could afford it. Lennon (his parents were huge Beatles fans) said he'd give her a break if she promised not to tell his gallery what she paid for it. A few years later, at another local exhibit, Melissa became absorbed with a painting by Lina Tharsing. It was a forest scene, painted with incredibly delicate brushwork, that depicted something that might have been a tent or might have been some kind of portal into a world beyond. I called up Lina and asked what she was asking for the painting. She offered me her "friend rate," but I said that painters needed to eat, and I paid full price (though not nearly what it was worth). That became Melissa's present for her fiftieth birthday. Since then, we have bought paintings and photographs by Guy Mendes, James Baker Hall, John Lackey, Frank Doring. I also inherited a couple of paintings by my mentor, Guy Davenport. Some of these artists you might have read about in *Oxford American* magazine, some of them you've never heard of.

Melissa and I are obviously not the Macklowes; our collection is not worth millions. I have no idea what it is worth monetarily. And I do not care. To pay millions for a work of art is to inevitably think of it as an "investment," and thus a commodity. The problem with that is that it ceases to be a work of art, an object of contemplation and nonmonetary enrichment. There is obviously no way to materially quantify the hours of enjoyment Melissa and I have received from looking at these individual works, painted by artists we have come to know and admire. I think of the Lorine Niedecker poem about an oil drum flanged to her small house. The poem begins, "I am sick with the Time's buying sickness," and ends: "true value expands / it warms." That seems to me exactly right. True value can never be a crass monetary value. The great American art critic Jerry Saltz, in "Zombies on the Walls," asked the question, Why does so much contemporary abstract art look the same? His answer: rich investors want art that looks exactly like all of their rich friends' art. The result is Saltz's hilarious portmanteau, "crapstraction"—"painters playing scales, doing finger exercises," making the equivalent of "visual Muzak." That's where the ideal of art-as-commodity leads us. But the kind of value Niedecker is talking about has a more immediate effect: it expands, it warms.

PAST MY NEIGHBOR'S field, as the path rises above the creek and back into the woods, the only other tracks I see are those of fox squirrels that descend down one fallen log, cross the trail momentarily, then climb up another log or root back into the safety of higher branches. I climb down to a break in the snow at the base of a large cherry tree. There, a small spring comes to life between two forked roots. I watch it gurgle up to the surface, then slowly crawl away into a small slough where a fox sparrow is drinking and flitting from stone to stone. There's always something both common and somehow miraculous about watching water rise up from hidden depths. Here's water when there wasn't any before; here's life making an unexpected appearance. And its transformations take place once more along the banks of the creek, where a thin shelf of ice follows the contours of the banks. In some places, looping, parallel lines wind through the ice like lines on a topographic map. In other places, the edge of the ice looks like a collection of small, transparent bones crushed together, fractal-like. A few inches above the surface of the creek, strange, biomorphic shapes hang from fallen limbs like clear, inverted mushrooms. And when I look up, the thinning clouds seem to be forming their own elliptical coastline. Everywhere I turn today, it seems, dihydrogen monoxide is performing its incredible, protean shifts from one state into another.

As I begin to grow hungry moving further along the trail, I think about the axis deer and antelope shoulder that is thawing on our cutting board right now, and I think of the two friends who hunted that meat, one in Maryland, one in Idaho. Their way of seeing the natural world is far different from mine. While I idly try to identify animal footprints in the snow, they see the world through a tracker's eyes. The markings and leavings of animals to them are a means to an end—namely, a good shot at a game animal. They come to the woods with a *purpose*—to return home with something to put in the freezer. I return home with a series of scribbled notes. They return home with dramatic stories of the hunt; I return to tell Melissa I saw a blue heron take flight or a snapping turtle dozing in the shallows. My friends have offered to teach me how to hunt, but since self-inflicted gun violence runs in my family, I've always kept my distance from firearms. Which isn't at all to say I won't relish and be grateful for the meat my friends have given me. Quite the opposite. I appreciate that their expertise will result in a meal I could not have procured. Nor do I think that their narrowly focused experience in the woods is in any way inferior to my more leisurely rambling. Perhaps we are simply tracking different quarry. They return with something of tangible interest to their families. What I return with is perhaps only of interest to me. Still, I think, we both return with a renewed, reinvigorated understanding of our own ways of being in the world.

The narcotic smell of wood smoke draws me trudging

back up the hillside. Finally back inside the house, I pull out our largest dutch oven and begin to cut up and brown the deer and antelope shoulder. Then I add in spices, garlic, and onion, followed by frozen okra, tomatoes, potatoes, and beans from our summer garden. Finally, I pour in Tabasco, Worcestershire, wine, and sherry. What I am making is Kentucky's signature soup, a hunter's stew called burgoo. It would traditionally have been cooked outdoors, over a fire and in a massive iron kettle. I've seen recipes that call for squirrel, rabbit, raccoon, even groundhog. As someone said about Scottish cuisine, burgoo sometimes seems like it was invented on a dare. But the truth is it's damn good—neither fish nor fowl, soup nor stew.

I let the burgoo simmer all day, and around dusk, Melissa makes some cornbread. We eat quietly at the table while we watch the trees' shadows grow long and almost blue against the snow in this, the day's last light.

SOLITUDE AND SOLIDARITY: in this country, we desperately need both but find neither.

TONIGHT, EARTH'S ONLY satellite rises like an ominous, barren hillside behind the eastern tree line. This is what astronomers, promoting their field of study, have come to call the *super blood wolf moon*, though it is in reality simply a lunar eclipse. But it's still quite a thing to see. This particular lunar eclipse finds said orb triangulating in perigee thirty thousand miles closer to Earth than usual, which makes it appear 30 percent brighter and 14 percent bigger. Throughout the evening, I make several treks up the lane to gauge the moon's trajectory up and over our woods and fields. Before the eclipse itself started, the shadows of the tress on the snow were as distinct as if the sun was hiding just behind some clouds. The moon rose higher and smaller into the sky. Now the stars are as numerous and revealing as I have seen them in some time. Orion's belt looks to be caught on the terminal branch of our spruce tree, and the twins of Gemini, my own sign, pulse in their contrapuntal nature beside the hunter, whose bow is aimed distinctly at Taurus. Then around midnight, the arc of Earth's umbra begins to creep over its neighbor's silvery surface. And when only a cusp of the corolla remains in sight, a crimson hue slowly but unmistakably begins to bleed over the moon. Our planet now stands squarely between it and the sun, and every sunrise and every sunset that spreads across the globe at this moment is casting their light over the moon. I lift my binoculars to my eyes, which are watering because of the cold. On the moon's surface, a deep maroon fills the water-less basins while an orange glow spreads over the highlands, and white rays shoot out from the Tycho crater. Apparently, the "wolf" part of the moon's appellation comes from the Algonquin, who called January's disc a canine moon. The same gravitational influence that the moon holds over Earth's tides also pulls the planet's human animals out of our warm houses to watch this strongest of tide-rising moons do its magnetic work. Like the wolf, we gaze up at this dead, distant thing with wonder. And I think we evolved, like the wolf, to feel this strange attachment to our loyal, solitary satellite. Even at 239,000 miles away, the moon—which our own early, gaseous planet probably flung into existence—remains inextricably part of who we are. Staring up at tonight's lunar phenomenon, I begin to feel more grounded on my own small globe drifting through the Milky Way. For some unexpected reason, I begin to feel more ontologically, even cosmically at home. I even feel suddenly proud of my blue planet and its companionable scarlet partner as they reel along through this ancient orbital dance around the sun, across the universe.

Were we standing on the moon tonight, we would see Earth tinged all around its circumference with a beautiful reddish-orange ring, which makes me think of the first photograph of our planet taken by the Apollo 8 astronaut William Anders fifty years ago this Christmas while he himself was orbiting the moon. In that photo, we can see the gray moonscape in the foreground and our own aqueous planet with swirling white clouds drifting alone against the blackest of backgrounds, the deepest of space. "We came all this way to explore the Moon," Anders later wrote, "and the most important thing is that we discovered the Earth." The image inspired poet Archibald MacLeish to write, "To see the Earth as it truly is, small and blue and beautiful in that eternal silence where it floats, is to see ourselves as riders on the Earth together, brothers on that bright loveliness in the eternal cold—brothers who know now that they are truly brothers." And sisters. In a solar system perhaps devoid of life, here we are—at least ten million species swimming, crawling, walking, and flying around a planet that is undeniably beautiful from space and undeniably beautiful on Earth in all of its particular biomes. Except from space, our divisions disappear. The distance of hundreds of thousands of miles gives us, we might say, perspective. It erases borders, cancels out countries. The only boundaries are natural ones: coastlines that demarcate landmasses and ridgelines that define watersheds. Race, religion, nationalities—these human inventions mean nothing. We are all heir to *Luca*, the Last Universal Common Ancestor, a single-cell organism that emerged four billion years ago when the earth was 560 million years old. What does that mean? It means we are all literally, genetically *kin*. All that remains ("all that remains!") is for our religions and our philosophies and our politicians to catch up with the already established fact of biological kinship. Biologically, evolutionarily, we rose from the one into the many. What Anders's photograph tells us is that, spiritually and ethically, we must now rise from the many into the one. And what *Luca* tells us is that the many *are* the one. You could call the one God, or you could call it Universal Mind, Buddha Nature, the All—it goes by many inadequate names. In the Gospel of Thomas, Jesus tells his followers, "On the day when you were one you became two. But when you become two, what will you do?" That, I believe, is *the* spiritual, philosophical, biological question. We know our evolutionary past, but we don't know our evolutionary future (neither does evolution). Yet our overwhelming human urge is to be reconciled with the one, either in death or in a (mystical) union in this life. Evangelical Christians, like the ones I grew up around, say we must be "born again" into that union with God. Mystics tell us the separation into two is only an illusion—that we are still part of the one, if only we could see it. Or we might say it this way: the Jesus we find in the Gospels understood the divinity (oneness) that resides inside us all (the many). Thus, Martin Luther King Jr. quoted theologian Paul Tillich to the effect that sin is separation. But both the separation and the sin are illusions. They only exist, I would argue, in a mind clouded by racial hatred or self-hated. Or both.

An American who first gleaned the implications that by viewing Earth from space, we might begin to understand our *oneness-in-diversity* ("brothers who know now that they are truly brothers") was the counterculture visionary and founder of the *Whole Earth Catalog*, Stewart Brand. In 1966, he was tripping on psychedelics in North Beach, San Francisco, when he had an idea: "If there were a picture of the whole Earth, man, that would change everything." Kinship would become apparent. It would be beautiful, man. He began preaching his plan on college campuses and hectoring NASA to release such an image. Two years later, the agency relented to Brand's grassroots movement and released a photo of the "whole Earth" (not just the partial "Earthrise" of William Anders's photo) taken by a satellite known as ATS-3. And Brand turned out to be right. Many Americans responded to that image the same way Archibald MacLeish responded to "Earthrise." They realized that our planet *was* amazing when seen from space, a jewel—a "blue marble"—hanging in a lifeless void. Maybe we should treat it as such and stop letting rivers like the Cuyahoga in Cleveland become so polluted that they actually catch on fire, as happened repeatedly. In 1970, the country celebrated its first Earth Day. That April 22 in Washington, DC, the event's fiery organizer, Denis Hayes, told a crowd, "Our country is stealing from poorer nations and from generations yet unborn. We seem to have a reverse King Midas touch. Everything we touch turns to garbage—142 million tons of smoke, 7 million junked cars, 30 million tons of paper, 28 billion bottles, 48 billion cans each year." Since then, of course, things have only gotten worse. Now human-induced climate change—or as Hayes might say, rich-countries-induced climate change—really is altering the fundamental dynamics of the planet, from bigger storms to more floods to melting ice to withering droughts and heat waves.

Around the same time that Hayes was issuing his lacerating jeremiads, the British scientist James Lovelock began pushing the case that our planet actually does act like a self-regulating, giant single organism that, over hundreds of millions of years, has regulated its own temperature for the good of all living and nonliving things. The atmosphere, he said, cycles carbon, hydrogen, nitrogen, oxygen, phosphorus, and sulfur to maintain relative climate homeostasis through stabilizing feedback loops. But now human beings are pumping carbon dioxide, methane, and other greenhouse gases into the atmosphere at a rate the planet hasn't seen in eight hundred thousand years. Nothing more drastically demonstrates our violation of the Stoic maxim to "live according to nature" than climate change. Like an invasive species, humans have become something the planet is struggling—and failing—to accommodate. In other words, it's the reverse Midas touch on a planetary scale.

Populations of wild animals have been *cut in half* since 1970, while human populations have doubled. There is no question that human beings are driving these animals to extinction with our own viruslike spread across the globe. But the question that should follow is, Are we driving ourselves extinct as well? The destruction of all that wild land is pushing wildlife closer and closer to humans, making the transmission of actual viruses ever more likely. Time and again through human history, we have tried to domesticate wildness, and in doing so, we have made it far easier—as COVID-19 has shown—for pathogens to domesticate *us* and put vast human populations at their mercy. Which is to say, pandemics coupled with climate change suggest that the answer to the extinction question may well be yes.

That then leads to a final question, at least in my mind: Would the rest of the world be better off without us? I think any cognizant human being would have to conclude that all the other (at least) ten million species on Earth would breathe a collective sigh of relief to see us go. Last month in my hometown, a man tied a one-year-old pit bull to his truck fender and dragged the dog for two blocks before bystanders forced him to stop. I would just as soon turn off that man's light as I would a light in my own house. Which is another way of saying, it wouldn't bother me in the least if the entire human race vanished from the face of the earth, along with its architecture and literature and military gunships. With each passing month, it becomes easier for me to *imagine* a world without human life. Of course, there would no longer be anyone around to appreciate Shakespeare or Chopin or the Watts Towers, but that would only be a loss to those of us who would no longer exist, which means it would be no loss at all. I say, let Silicon Valley techno-futurists and their AI acolytes shed this mortal coil, upload their brains to a computer, and send it to Mars. Good riddance. Good riddance to us all.

Of course, our species' leaving would be tragic: tragic in the Greek sense of *hubris*—that we would deserve it—but also tragic in that it would be accompanied by appalling human suffering before we vanished: water wars, famines, heat death, viral deaths, refugees brutalized at closed borders. But that is the future toward which we are hurtling our species unless we are able, as the poet Robinson Jeffers wrote, to "uncenter our minds from ourselves." If we do, as a species, survive the coming catastrophe, I suspect it will only be as the small bands of resourceful, food-sharing generalists that Paul Shepard describes in his classic plea *Coming Home to the Pleistocene*. I strongly suspect the only things that will sustain us in the future are the kind of watershed communities and economies I described earlier. Heat-absorbing concrete, heat-induced violence, and viruses will make densely crowded cities unlivable. The desk-based skills of most urban dwellers will prove useless in that future. Instead, we might possibly return to our rightful genetic home where we lived for half a million years before agriculture brought on the modern world and all of its maladies a mere ten thousand years ago. We will need a society organized around work that truly needs to get done—and climate change will force us into one. I may be a democratic-socialist-eco-anarcho-syndicalist, but I'm not fighting for any ideology. It's too late for that—too late to overthrow the system. The system is going to overthrow itself. Climate change and pandemics will make sure of that. They will be the great levelers. In the meantime, in the decades ahead of us, I believe we must firmly adopt what James Baldwin called the tragic view of life. In his fittingly titled *The Fire Next Time*, Baldwin says we humans invent mosques, churches, and blood sacrifices to deny the simple fact of death. In a similar way, today we have erected a towering politics and a fundamentalist religion of denial so we can ignore climate change, viral pandemics, and the thought of our own disappearance. But they all amount to the same thing: fear of personal death and fear of species death. The only response to that, writes Baldwin, is to take responsibility for life as we find it, a life that is a preparation for death. "One must negotiate this passage as nobly as possible," he writes, "for the sake of those who are coming after us." This seems crucial to me. We must navigate the years to come with as much dignity, courage, and empathy as we can muster. It could be tragic, but the remaining beauty of the natural world might sustain our spirits, and a dormant human nobility—the kind we often see after natural disasters—might be awakened to help us meet our fate.

IT IS FIFTEEN degrees this morning when I go out to refill the chickens' watering stand, the one with an electric heater attached at the base. My reward is nine eggs nestled in one corner on a bed of straw. These hens haven't laid in two cold, gray weeks, but I gather up the eggs, tuck them in the pockets of my barn jacket, and go up to the house to make breakfast for Melissa, who's sleeping in. I layer slices of ham and avocado on rafts of toast, then set the fried eggs on top, a sort of eggs Benedict. The orange yokes are so rich, a Hollandaise sauce would almost be redundant.

Today is Martin Luther King Jr. Day, and to mark the occasion, Melissa has published a fine opinion piece in the *Louisville Courier-Journal*, not that anyone knows it. Melissa is a policy analyst for Kentucky's Council for Postsecondary Education, and one of her many jobs is to ghostwrite pieces to which her boss, the council's president, can then affix his name. In her op-ed, Melissa argued that Dr. King believed education was the surest path to both social mobility and self-fulfillment. She quoted him as saying, "To think incisively and to think for one's self is very difficult. We are prone to let our mental life become invaded by legions of half-truths, prejudices and propaganda. . . . To save man from the morass of propaganda, in my opinion, is one of the chief aims of education." God knows we are more surrounded than ever by those digital legions, and teaching American students, at any level, to think for themselves becomes more crucial, even as it becomes more difficult. Melissa pointed out that in Kentucky, the college-going rate for Black students is 7 percent lower than the state average, and she argued for more affordability, better high school preparation, and universities that are friendlier to adults returning to school.

After breakfast, I build a fire in the woodstove, we move our chairs closer to the heat, and we settle in for what Melissa calls "a lazy day of reading." Spurred by her op-ed, I decide to revisit Martin Luther King Jr.'s "Letter from Birmingham Jail." In an age so devoid of rhetorical elegance, so relentlessly shrill, it's a lesson in subtlety and surgical persuasion—an essay that bears returning to again and again.

The events in Birmingham in 1963 crystalized for King the necessity of nonviolent civil disobedience over simply making moral appeals to the consciences of southern whites. "If you create enough tension, you attract attention to your cause," King reasoned. And it was the events in Birmingham that finally got the attention of John and Robert Kennedy and led to the March on Washington later that year. A year earlier, students at Miles College organized a boycott of Birmingham's downtown businesses because they refused to hire Black people or let them sit at lunch counters. As president of the Southern Christian Leadership Conference, King was frustrated that, since the Montgomery bus boycott, he had not been able to secure for his cause the attention of the national media or even the majority of what he called "white moderates." Birmingham looked like an opportunity to dramatize the humiliations of segregation and the need for federal civil rights legislation. Under the sway of the Ku Klux Klan, the city had become so violent that Black residents referred to it as "Bombingham." A movement quickly formed there, with the goal of abolishing discriminatory hiring while desegregating lunch counters, restrooms, and fitting rooms. During a demonstration on April 7, Birmingham's public safety commissioner, Bull Connor, unleashed snarling German shepherds onto the crowd. The city convinced a circuit judge to issue an injunction against all future marches or protests. On Good Friday, an apprehensive King appeared before his fellow SCLC lieutenants in overalls, prepared to be arrested. The small group began walking toward city hall in what King called a prayer pilgrimage, but four blocks into the march, a paddy wagon appeared, and everyone was carted off to jail.

To King's frustration, Black adults in Birmingham had been slow to join his demonstrations, but now, Black high school students poured into the streets. Connor brought back the dogs, but he also unleashed the pummeling force of fire hoses that ripped clothes off protesters and pressed them up against brick walls. (In 2010, the visual artist Theaster Gates created a work called *Flag*. It consists of different, multicolored fire hoses sewn to a canvas in vertical strips, like an American flag. When Melissa and I first saw the piece, we stared at it for a very long time. "*This*," she finally said, "is the kind of art I want to see.") During Easter weekend, photos from the scene were disseminated across the front pages of the nation's newspapers. As one member of the SCLC remarked, "We had calculated for the stupidity of a Bull Connor." Another member exclaimed, "We've got a movement. We've got a movement."

Back at the jail, King had been placed in solitary confinement and prevented from communicating with his lawyers. So instead, he got down to work on a long letter. It was a response to another letter—signed by four bishops, three Protestant ministers, and a rabbi—that had just appeared in the local newspaper. They called on King to end his non-violent resistance in Birmingham and let the courts settle the issue of integration. King began writing his letter in the margins of the newspaper, then on scrap sheets "supplied by a friendly Negro trustee," and finally on a pad provided by his attorneys. "Letter from Birmingham Jail" appeared a month later in a pamphlet published by the American

Friends Service Committee, a Quaker group that had been fighting racism since the 1920s.

Eighty years later, what seems so impressive to me about King's letter is his agility at engaging an adversary. In an age where we seem to only yell at or past those with whom we disagree, King's approach is masterful and something, I think, we might learn from. For one thing, he accepts the eight clergymen as "men of genuine good will" and begins from there. We might say, as I have said to my own writing students, that this is simply a smart rhetorical move—a way of engaging one's audience. And it is that, but I think it's also a way *to be heard*. King never doubts the other men's motives or their consciences. He never questions their status as men of God. In other words, he never threatens them with his own (obvious) moral high ground. Rather, King says, in essence, I've patiently listened to your point of view, so please extend the same courtesy to me. He knows their grievances and reminds them that he knows: he's an outside agitator, his work is "untimely," he breaks laws, he precipitates violence, he's an extremist. Then he proceeds to methodically address and dismantle these claims. Precipitating violence? Isn't that like blaming a man who just got robbed for having some money on him? Extremism? Wasn't Jesus an extremist for love, and while we're on that subject, wasn't he also an "outside agitator," stirring up the Roman cities of Palestine with his message of extreme love? Untimeliness? History is a long tragic story dramatizing the fact that a privileged majority seldom willingly gives up that privilege. "We know through painful experience that freedom is never voluntarily given by the oppressor," writes King; "it must be demanded by the oppressed." Which brings us to lawbreaking and direct nonviolent action. The latter, for King and the SCLC, involved four steps: the collection of facts to determine whether injustices exist, negotiation, self-purification, and finally, direct action. When negotiation fails, one must train oneself in nonviolent resistance and then act. If that action breaks a law, one must ask if the law being broken is just or unjust. If it is deemed unjust—if it "degrades human personality" and "gives the segregator a false sense of superiority and the segregated a false sense of inferiority"—then it must be broken. Writes King: "An individual who breaks a law that conscience tells him is unjust, and willingly accepts the penalty by staying in jail to arouse the conscience of the community over its injustice, is in reality expressing the very highest respect for the law."

I offer this quick and inadequate summary of King's letter because it always amazes me how many Americans I meet who haven't read it. Everyone has heard the "I Have a Dream" speech, but that was a performance—a brilliant one; the country was never the same after it. But it wasn't the model for all American rhetoric of persuasion going forward that the "Letter" is. In my opinion, its only rival is James Baldwin's excoriating book-length essay *The Fire Next Time*. The two men had much in common. Both were raised in the Black Christian church and both had fathers (and in King's case, grandfathers) who were ministers. But Baldwin, who became a child preacher in Harlem, was the son of a menacing father with schizophrenia. To escape his father's rage, Baldwin left home early, abandoned the church, and became a freelance writer who, unlike King, had no formal education. And unlike King, Baldwin's own inherited anger and disgust extended to the Black church as well as the white. American Christianity, in his view (and in mine), bred a pacifism whereby modern Christians prayed for salvation from this world but did nothing to make it better. Toward the end of his preaching career, Baldwin said it took all of his strength not tell his congregation to "throw away their Bibles and get off their knees and go home and organize, for example, a rent strike."

For Baldwin, there was a profound contradiction at the core of Christianity. The message of Jesus—*Do unto others as you would have them do unto you*—had been hijacked by "the mercilessly fanatical and self-righteous St. Paul." As a result, this history of Christianity was one of "unmitigated arrogance and cruelty," an "indispensable justification for the planting of the flag." It was a Christian, after all, who brought some African to this country in chains, gave him the name "Baldwin," and forced him to bow down at the foot of a cross. In the end, decided Baldwin, the only way to lead a moral life was to abandon any Christian church, Black or white. But as the relentless argument of *The Fire Next Time* unfolds, something rather amazing happens. Though Baldwin never admits to it explicitly, he inserts his own secret gospel into his attack on Christianity. That is to say, he *reclaims* the true message of its founder and makes it his own message for America if it ever hopes for atonement and release from a history of violence and hypocrisy. Hate, he writes, is a mask "we fear we cannot live without and know we cannot live within." Love, "as a state of being," is the only force that can unmask the tragic lives of all men and women. Rejecting the teaching of Elijah Muhammad, Baldwin writes that he would "oppose any attempt that Negroes may make to do unto others what has been done to them." Then, giving a second twist to the golden rule, he submits: "*Whoever debases others is debasing himself.*" That was what the white American, the white Christian, had to finally learn. That first Black Baldwin had no choice in coming to America. But James Baldwin had no choice but to remain. He wasn't an African and he wasn't going back to Africa. And to invent a mythic past, as the Nation of Islam did, was foolish in his opinion. However unforgivably this county had treated him, he had no choice in the end but to be an American. And white America had no choice but to accept him. Their destinies, like their pasts, were inextricably linked. Only by truly admitting that, would we, in Baldwin's famous phrase, "achieve our country."

Baldwin wrote *The Fire Next Time* the same year King wrote "A Letter from Birmingham Jail"—1963. I find that rather astonishing. Out of a cauldron of national division, distrust, and violence came these voices of empathy and purpose—voices that more than anything else showed a way forward.

There are actually two versions of King's "Letter." The longer one, the one I am reading now, appeared in his book *Why We Can't Wait*, and it levels much more condemnation at the white church than does the original. In it, he remembers many ministers rationalizing their acquiescence to segregation by saying, "Those are social issues with which the Gospel has no real concern"—a position that, as Baldwin also knew, ignores basically everything Jesus taught. And

King admits in the later version that when he drove past beautiful churches in the South, he wondered, "Who worships here? Who is their God?"

I think about my grandfather's church in rural Achilles, Virginia. It was a plain brick structure with a high white steeple. When I was a child and my mother and I went to visit my grandparents after the death of my father, Don, the two of us would play a game of who could spot the steeple first over the tall Virginia pines. At the back of the church's baptistery was an inept rendering of a thoroughly anglicized Jesus. And the plaster walls of the sanctuary were as white as its congregation. When I got older and my grandfather was retired from preaching, he revealed to me his decades-old plan for what he would have done had a Black person attempted to worship at the First Baptist Church of Achilles: "I simply would have said the benediction and dismissed the congregation immediately." I can't remember what my response to this was, but I'm sure it's nothing that would have impressed Dr. King. Later, I asked my mother if this had been my father's solution to segregating the church as well. "No," she said. "When I asked Don about it once, he said, 'I would never do that.'"

When my uncle, my father's brother, died in 2007, there were few mourners at the funeral and fewer at the graveside. Like Baldwin's father, my uncle had been mentally ill for a long time and had finally driven away or abandoned his few friends. My grandparents were dead, and most of their friends who might have attended had also passed away. I myself was out of the country, but my mother tells me that as she and my stepfather watched the casket lowered, a car she didn't recognize pulled up. Two Black women—one in her sixties, the other her adult daughter, approached the grave. They said a prayer. My parents looked on but said nothing. After the interment was complete, the older woman took my mother aside and told her that thirty years earlier, she and my uncle Dan had been lovers.

After my father died, my grandfather decided that my grandmother needed something to do with her grief. So he set her up as the director of the Friendship House, a Baptist-affiliated organization that offered after-school and summer programming for children of color in a poor part of Newport News. My grandmother had an office on the third floor of the large old house and basically oversaw the books and signed the checks. My uncle started volunteering at the Friendship House as well. That's where he met Mary. They started to see each other on the sly, or at least unbeknownst to my grandparents and the rest of our family.

Then Mary got pregnant. She and Dan went to see my grandfather at his church office. They told him the situation and said they wanted to get married. No one in the family knows exactly what my grandfather said to them. We do know that he forbade it. He convinced Dan and Mary that such a union would ruin our family's reputation in the community and jeopardize his own position as pastor of a white church in conservative, rural Virginia.

Dan was, of course, a full-grown man who didn't need his father's consent for anything. But my grandfather wielded the same psychic power, the same domineering force over my uncle that he did over my father. Dan backed down, acquiesced. Mary said she was going to have the baby anyway.

My grandfather bought her off. He purchased a house for her; maybe there were other payments along the way as well. My mother isn't sure. But we do know Dan kept seeing Mary and her daughter for years to come. My mother said it suddenly made sense to her why at every family holiday, my uncle left immediately after dinner and didn't return until well into the early morning.

Finally, Mary gave him an ultimatum: either marry her or forfeit any more opportunities to see his daughter. But Dan, who we know was in love with Mary, couldn't do it; he couldn't step up. The specter of my grandfather's disapproval was still too much, still too debilitating.

Mary and her daughter moved away from Newport News, settled in South Carolina. Mary told my mother that she never saw my uncle again. But like my father, he began to fall apart. He signed up for the Coast Guard, but during a training exercise, Dan dove into a pool and refused to rise to the surface. Divers had to drag his body out and resuscitate him. He was discharged. Other suicide attempts followed. My grandmother was understandably frantic that she might lose another son, but my grandfather began to build a distance between himself and Dan. In his mind, the wrong son had died and the surviving one had been only a disappointment. I know this because my grandfather never tried to hide it, never tried to assure Dan of any filial affection.

My uncle became more and more erratic. He couldn't hold jobs, and he began to exhibit the same bipolar behavior that plagued his brother, my father. For decades to come, his doctors never succeeded in finding the right combination of medications to quiet his demons. Once, he disappeared for months and was found wandering a roadside in Arizona, unrecognizable to himself. So Dan wouldn't end up homeless, my grandmother drew one concession from my grandfather—that he bequest to Dan their house in their will. My grandfather did that and nothing else.

Dan did marry late in life and was supported by his wife's pension. And then he died. And then the woman my grandfather wouldn't let him marry appeared at his grave. Then just as quickly, she and her daughter disappeared from our lives.

When I visited Dan's grave years later, I caught sight of the white cross that still sits atop the white steeple of the church my grandfather once pastored. Who worships there? I wondered. Who is their god?

As I WAS feeding the woodstove today, I found a dead wren wedged between two logs at the bottom of my woodpile. No doubt the below-zero temperatures of the last few nights stopped its heart. Millions of wrens die this way each winter. Still, it seems no small thing to hold in my palm this particularly lifeless bird with its umber breast and brown plumage. The Gospels tell us that God knows when every sparrow falls. If that is indeed the case, he must keep busy with such tabulations, given that 13.7 million birds die each day in this country alone. Bird populations in the US and Canada have fallen 28 percent since 1970. There are now *three billion* fewer birds. In North America, *Homo sapiens*, the species supposedly created in God's image, is responsible for the better part of that dying off due to its domesticated cats, tall buildings, pesticides, and propensity for habitat destruction.

One-fourth of the 836 species covered by the Migratory Bird Treaty Act are in serious decline, according to the Audubon Society. But since that 1918 law took none of these contemporary causes into consideration, and since it certainly doesn't prohibit them now, the statute is virtually meaningless. And every avian species in decline is a coal mine canary—warning us of our own demise. We do not live in a fallen world because we have sinned; on the contrary, our most modern sin is that we are causing so much of the world to fall. Birds are falling, forests are falling, mountains are falling. We have exiled the holy from this world so we can turn its "resources" into money as quickly as possible. Our most modern sin is that we do not love the world enough. It is a kind of spiritual death.

The Gospel story of the fallen sparrow is supposed to make us humans feel more secure in our standing with God: if he cares even for the sparrows, think how much more God cares about us. But unfortunately, that sense of our own self-importance has only led to the death of billions of sparrows as we build ever greater monuments to ourselves. We have taken a saying meant to assuage our existential anxieties and turned it into a license for hubris, for making godlike attempts to alter the natural world. That's what I keep thinking as I stare down at this dead wren. That's why I reject the Christian idea of some separate anthropomorphic deity in favor of the Stoics' belief that the creator is simultaneously the creation. Because if the world is diminished by the death of one small songbird, then so is its god.

THE EXPOSED ORANGE roots of the hedge apple tree snake across the trail a few feet from the creek. Folded beneath one long root, I find this poem by the Reclusive Socialist:

Icicles hang like fangs
from the wild grapevine
that loops down in front
of a limestone cliff face,

a sinister grin,
a withering look

I understand at once.
Walking this grey gorge for years,
I have learned to read the signs.
It means the god of forgiveness
is gone,

        tired
        of his faithless charges.

Now only this obdurate rock
will remain
to judge us,

will reflect back
as little mercy
as we ourselves
could manage.

For years to come
the cliff face will wear
this pitiless smile

while it watches us
disappear

like islands of melting ice
that still bear
the banks' faint outline.

I feel the Reclusive Socialist's poetry growing darker and darker. Is it contributing to my own gathering dread?

ICE CRYSTALS PRESS against the windows like calcified ginkgo leaves, fossils drained of color but preserved by winter's ruthlessness. A furious snowstorm blows sideways from the West, slamming screen doors and scattering dark-eyed juncos. I hunker down beside the fire with my dogs. The flames inside the stove dance in quick runs along a flutelike branch. And like my favorite music, they give off heat and even burn if you get close enough. So I drop the needle on some late Billie Holiday. Her voice, hollowed out by heroin, sounds like a cave of pain, a bird with a broken wing trying to find its way to the end of every song. And I'm struck once again by the way beauty and pain can reside in such close proximity. Perhaps they need one another. The pain needs the beauty to keep from drowning in itself. The beauty needs the pain to keep it from drifting up into an airy nothingness. One grounds the other while one holds the other up—just above rock bottom.

THROUGHOUT THESE PAGES, I have been drawing on two schools of Hellenistic philosophy, Epicureanism and Stoicism, which flourished between the death of Alexander the Great in 323 BCE and the defeat of Mark Antony and Cleopatra at the Battle of Actium in 32 BCE. Each of these schools has become fundamental to my own way of thinking because they ground me at once in the solitary, the social, and the natural realm of *this world*, no other.

Because Epicurus defined the greatest good as *happiness* and the Stoics defined it as *virtue*, the two philosophies are generally thought to be at odds. Yet on closer inspection, acting virtuously makes a Stoic happy, while pursuing the happiness of oneself and others makes the Epicurean virtuous. Cooperating with other Epicureans ensures both their happiness and yours because such reciprocity more likely ensures that needs get met on both ends of the exchange. And contrary to popular belief, the Stoics had no opposition to happiness, so long as pursuing it didn't compromise one's character. As for the Epicureans, if the pursuit of pleasure caused someone pain, then it wasn't real pleasure because it couldn't be had with a clean conscience. Still, we might say that Epicureanism, which began in a private garden, is largely a private philosophy, while Stoicism, which began in a public colonnade, is both a philosophy of the self and a call to the larger social good. Epicurus taught his students not to fear death, as well as how to avoid mental anguish through self-sufficient modesty and the rejection of

insatiable cravings. The Stoics emphasized four Socratic virtues: wisdom, self-control, courage, and justice. The first two are extensions of the self, while the second two carry the self into the sphere of empathy and fellow feeling. While the earlier Greek Stoics, for whom only fragments of their writings have survived, divided their teaching into logic, physics, and ethics, the Roman Stoics put most of their emphasis on an ethic made manifest through action. What it all amounts to, said the Stoic Roman Emperor, Marcus Aurelius, is a "well-ordered spirit."

In his *Meditations*, probably composed in solitude on the Danube during a military campaign, Marcus wrote, "If you are distressed by anything external, the pain is not due to the thing itself but to your own estimate of it; and this you have the power to revoke at any moment. If the cause of the trouble lies in your own character, set about reforming your principles; who is there to hinder you?" For the

Stoics, nothing external (such as money or fame) is inherently good or bad. Only one's character can be good, can be virtuous, can display integrity. And that character, ultimately, is the *only thing* within our means to control. Thus, we have control over our own actions but not over the outcome of those actions. So much of our unhappiness, said the Stoics, is tied to those external outcomes that we can't control. The candidate we voted for (an action) didn't win (the outcome). According to the Stoics, we can fret and fume over that, curse our fellow citizens for their thickheadedness, or we can choose to not let that outcome overly upset us, since we can't do anything about it anyway (and if we can, we should). The encompassing Stoic claim for achieving contentment is to decide what we can control and what we cannot. Once that decision is made, we do our best with the parts of our lives we can determine. This is where the Stoics found personal contentment. They took the hardships that befell them and put those hardships to use. "What stands in the way becomes the way," Marcus writes. Or, advises Epictetus, consider yourself a character in a play. You can't control what happens to your character—that's already been decided by the playwright—but you can still act the part with great artistry and feeling.

The one thing we can always control is our own response to a situation, what Marcus calls our "estimate" of it. We can realize that what most affects us about an external event is not the event itself but our judgment of it—and that, unlike some events, is something we can control. Therefore, we can always act according to our own sense of character and integrity. Thus, the Stoic "sage" is perfectly free because she (the Stoics were the only ancient school to accept women into their ranks) only desires what is within her means of achieving. Though we can't control outcomes, we can control the way we let those outcomes affect us, and given the sorry state of our national politics, Stoicism seems to me a very relevant philosophy for our times. Which is to say, I have no leverage over legislators who refuse to acknowledge human-induced climate change, but I can plant a lot of trees to, in some small way, mitigate their poor decisions, and I can encourage others to help plant more trees. In this sense, theologian Reinhold Niebuhr's 1934 "Serenity Prayer" is a perfect distillation of Stoicism:

> God, grant me the serenity to accept the things I
>   cannot change,
> Courage to change the things I can,
> And the wisdom to know the difference.

The Stoics coined the word *cosmopolitan* to mean, not a city dweller as we understand the term today, but rather, in Epictetus's phrase, "a citizen of the Universe." Stoicism's founder, Zeno, said we could overcome prejudice and xenophobia by considering foreigners not as members of a different nation or state but as fellow citizens of the world. I think back to what poet Archibald MacLeish said when he looked at the first photos of Earth from space, that we are "brothers on that bright loveliness in the eternal cold—brothers who know now that they are truly brothers." The counterpart to Stoic individual equanimity was a social magnanimity ("greatness of soul") that reached out to other human beings, to animals, and to the natural world. Thus, the Stoics' most cherished maxim, *zen kata physin*, "live according to nature," resonated on three interdependent levels: live according to one's own inner nature, live according to the evolutionary social nature that binds human to human through cooperation, and live according to the greater biological and cosmological world, knowing that all life came from one common ancestor. All three *natures* reinforce one another in ways that are at once poetic, ethical, and biological. "Think often of the bond that unites all things in the universe," writes Marcus, "and their dependence upon one another." It's certainly true that Charles Darwin forced us to abandon the Stoic belief that nature is ruled by "Reason," but Marcus's notion that all life is of one substance and is as interdependent as the limbs of a body remains biologically sound. Darwin also showed us that, like our closest genetic kin, the bonobo ape, we are intensely social creatures who have evolved traits like shame and envy that ensure we remain enmeshed in the social fabric. The Stoics believed that since we are innately social, we must hone our sense of wisdom, courage, and justice for the benefit of the greater good. And that greater good includes all living things. Another Darwinian lesson the Stoics would have commended is the biological realization that *Homo sapiens* does not stand atop a hierarchy of animal life but is simply another (certainly interesting) species in a vast constellation of species.

What attracts me most to Stoicism—more than to any other Western school of philosophy—is the way it makes synonymous *thinking*, *being*, and *doing*. The Stoics didn't, like Plato or Kant or Descartes, privilege the life of the mind over that of the body. Philosophy for the Stoics was not a way of thinking through metaphysical or epistemological problems; it was at once a kind of personal therapy (being) and a call to ethical action (doing). The Stoics rejected the Platonic system of universal truths and essentialist definitions. The laws of nature were the laws of the gods—as simple as that. Virtue can exist without being a universal good. We just decide for ourselves as a community what we want it to look like. Great tomes did not have to be written on the theory of justice, for instance. For the Stoics and Epicureans, a contingent definition of justice was simply: do no harm and don't be harmed. All manner of practical decisions could and can—with some obvious dissension and debate—be based on that criteria.

I find in Stoicism a strong connection to the Four Noble Truths and the Eightfold Path of Buddhism. Both reject absolute truths and emphasize the world's transitory nature. Both emphasize that human suffering is caused by the way we misperceive our place in the world, the way we project selfish desires onto things beyond our control. Once we diagnose the problem—suffering, or *dukkha*, caused by craving, or "thirst"—we can begin work on a pragmatic course of treatment that might lead to *nirvana*, the "extinction of thirst," the extinction of the grasping self. And the Eightfold Path, like Stoicism, offers a way to transcend the self-serving ego and find contentment in one's life through right understanding of things as they really are, right thought of compassion, right speech that avoids slander and malice, right action that promotes ethical conduct, right livelihood that doesn't profit at others' expense, and right mindfulness that pays attention to the present and doesn't get lost in destructive judgments. For Stoics, like Zen Buddhists, the past and the future are of no concern because we can do nothing about them. What's done is done, and what hasn't happened yet is unknowable. Therefore, all attention, and all efforts to act honorably, must be focused in and on the present. And as in Buddhism, that attention (*prosoche*) was the fundamental Stoic spiritual attitude and spiritual exercise. Because all of life is a Heraclitean river we never step in twice, this focus on the present also becomes a reminder of life's, and the self's, impermanence. That realization, said the Buddha and the Stoics, should teach us humility and compassion.

Yet having said all that, in the end, I don't believe Buddhism is a philosophy that I, as a westerner, could or should try to appropriate. There are finally too many foreign concepts—*sunyata*, for instance—that my Western mind isn't wired to fully comprehend. But I do feel comfortable claiming the Hellenistic tradition as my own, as something I come from and understand at the level of its language, its history, and its ideas. What's more, it's a philosophy that makes profound sense to me, sitting alone by a stream in the Inner Bluegrass or planting trees at an abandoned strip mine on the Cumberland Plateau.

MY FAVORITE CHURCH, if one can call it that, stands in New Harmony, Indiana. Built by the architect Philip Johnson, the Roofless Church is essentially two massive wooden doors and four brick walls, open to the heavens. A wood-shingled baldachin stands as a kind of altar and takes the form of an upturned rosebud. The Roofless Church is every-one's church, everyone under the sun. Or put another way (for the last time), it is a place to worship Spinoza's God-or-Nature. It's model, one supposes, was the ancient, "hypae-thral" Egyptian temples that also opened onto the skies. In his journal, Thoreau spoke of wanting to write a "hypae-thral or unroofed book, lying open under the ether and per-meated by it, open to all weathers, not easy to be kept on a shelf." I too wanted to write such a book here and hope that I have, on some level, succeeded. Much of it was written outside, and I like to imagine the book lying open—like a pond beneath a clear sky—offering a psalm of praise to all the living things reflected within it.

As I read back over these pages, I realize there may seem a kind of dissonance between my grim prediction of American democracy unraveling while climate change pushes our spe-cies toward extinction, and my utopian dreams of decentral-ized, radically egalitarian watershed cantons. Do I support Robinson Jeffers's philosophy of "inhumanism"—his re-jection of "human solipsism and recognition of the trans-human magnificence" of the larger animal world? Or do I hold out some hope for Martin Luther King Jr.'s determined belief in the arc of human progress? F. Scott Fitzgerald fa-mously remarked that "the test of a first-rate intelligence is the ability to hold two opposing ideas in mind at the same time and still retain the ability to function." I have no idea where my own intelligence ranks, but I am trying to balance both possibilities—both futures—in my mind at once. Put another way, I am trying to balance the probability of eco-logical and species catastrophe with the slim chance that we might thread the bottleneck and emerge better, more cooperative social animals. Fitzgerald went on to say, "One should, for example, be able to see that things are hopeless yet be determined to make them otherwise." I too am trying to reject what has come to seem a rather fatuous notion—*hope*—while still clinging to the possibility of human *integrity* and *resolve*. Based on the intransigence of old, white US senators and the leviathan churning of the capitalist machine, I do not believe that we, as a species, will "solve" the climate crisis. What's so infuriating about this is that we *could* solve it, or at least could have about a decade ago. We already possess, and possessed then, the technology and the scientific understanding to achieve the Paris Climate Agreement's goal of limiting global temperature rise to 1.5 degrees Celsius by 2050. It would happen something like this: All energy services would need to be powered by electricity, which would have to be powered by something other than coal and gas. Solar power could make up nearly one-third of that energy. Wind could power another third. Hydroelectric could account for 10 percent of that equation, along with geothermal heat, underwater turbines, synthetic fuels, and the possibility of nuclear fusion. What else could we do to achieve the 1.5-degree goal? Replace deforestation with reforestation, feed cattle seaweed to cut their methane production by 99 percent (or better yet, grow meat in labs), reduce fertilizer (and thus nitrous oxide) through crop rotation and the spreading of biochar on agricultural fields, and use carbon capture and sequestration to cut emissions from cement and steel production. Problem—theoretically—solved.

This is obviously an oversimplification, but not by much. The economic problems have already been solved: in 80 percent of the world, renewable energy is now cheaper than coal, oil, and gas. In terms of sheer dollars, the US military spends $766 billion dollars a year, 40 percent of all global military spending. Global military spending tops out at around $2 trillion. Split that in half, and most estimates say you would have enough money to address the most drastic elements of climate change. My point being, we have the *ability* to stop a climate catastrophe; what we do not have is the *will*, the moral fortitude. Technological progress we understand. Moral progress we do not. To hit 1.5 degrees Celsius by 2050, carbon emissions would have to be cut in half over the next decade, then fall by 15 percent every year until they hit zero. This simply is not going to happen. That's the reality. Another reality is that one political party in this country has no interest in protecting their grandchildren, while the captains of industry have no interest in forgoing profits in the name of the common good. Thus, there is a realistic and resigned hemisphere of my brain that says the change we need to stave off climate catastrophe isn't coming. But there is another hemisphere that refuses to acquiesce, that can still imagine a life of beauty and dignity for both individuals and communities, even as the world burns.

So here are two other opposing ideas we need to balance in our minds. One idea is that nothing substantial can be done about climate change unless decisions are made on an international level by nation-states themselves. The other idea is that individual actions do matter. Both, I think, are true. For there to be any kind of inhabitable future, all countries must make serious reduction pledges and stick to them (right now, almost no country does the latter). But it's also true that US emissions have fallen 20 percent since 2005, almost all due to local and voluntary actions by citizens, businesses, and municipalities. As suggested earlier, I think planting trees is one of the most important and effective acts an individual can undertake to fight climate change. There are, of course, many others. But to take individual actions is always a social stance as well. It at least puts us on the right side—the side of the solution. Then our actions reverberate with other individuals, because those other individuals see us making a deliberate attempt to change the world for the better (and no change is quite as literal, as obvious, or as gratifying as planting a tree). Thus, those other individuals might resort to action as well. And when we are done taking some climate-ameliorating action, we have a story to tell about it—a hypocrisy-proof tale that might also convince others to join our cause. Generosity and good will are just as socially contagious as anger and resentment. Our story isn't a political debate but rather a demonstration of our own values, and no value system is more convincing than one that has been put into action. I was once fortunate enough to witness a commencement speech by the Irish poet and Nobel laureate Seamus Heaney. He concluded his remarks by saying there is no reason to totally despair about the world if we know there is good work to do and we are willing to do it. I've thought about that quite a bit over the last twenty years. I still retain for myself what James Baldwin called the tragic view of life. Rather than fear death, writes

Baldwin, one should "*earn* one's death by confronting with passion the conundrum of life." That is something we certainly can do in the face of climate change and the suffering it will bring. We can fight for life—*all* life—even while we watch it disappear. One can still embrace—indeed, one *must* embrace—the tragic view of life with great vigor, expansiveness, and courage. In his poem, "The Oven Bird," Robert Frost writes of this wood warbler:

> The bird would cease and be as other birds
> But that he knows in singing not to sing.
> The question that he frames in all but words
> Is what to make of a diminished thing?

The first thing I make of a diminished thing is that it is still a thing, an organic, cellular constitution of vitality. There may be no more mastodons in Kentucky, but there are bears and foxes and otters. There are sunfish and herons and owls. These neighbors and their habitats are still worth protecting; that's the second thing I make of the ovenbird's query. My final response is that by diminishing the world, we diminish ourselves. To think of the self as only a fortress of molecules separated off from all other beings is indeed a diminished point of view, and a sad one. We only overcome our personal fear and anger—which are, after all, the same thing—when we stop seeing the world as a competition between winners and losers and understand it instead as a teeming constellation of subjects, which are all finally part of a larger self—of Lynn Margulis's symbiotic microcosm. We badly need to begin cultivating this way of seeing our roles in life's drama. It's simply a far richer way to understand the world and our place in it.

I have long thought that our "inner landscapes" of the heart-mind tend to be reflections of our outer landscapes. That is to say, there's a reason that the people of Eastern Kentucky suffer from—worse than anywhere else in the country—depression, violence, ill health, and substance abuse. And the reason is the strip mines that have ravaged the mountains all around them—polluting the rivers and streams and sending extracted wealth out of the region. The same Gallup study that found Eastern Kentucky at the rock bottom of its well-being index found that residents of Utah scored highest, largely because they derive much satisfaction from exploring the wild, natural landscapes of the West. Our breaths, literally, connect our inner and outer landscapes, and when one is damaged—by coal dust, say—so will be the other. But the breath is also the philosophical *pneuma* that connects our individual selves (the many) with the larger self (the one) that we can call God or Brahman or the Cosmos. To allow our individual selves to shed the defensive parameters of ego—to ride the breath out of the body—would mean to be released into the larger "stream of consciousness," where the inner landscape merges with, and is reflected in, the landscape of the natural world. Self-consciousness would blossom into consciousness of the world beyond ourselves.

The breath carries these two selves, these two landscapes, back and forth—the microcosm reflecting and interpenetrating the macrocosm. In fact, for William James, there was no difference between an inner and outer landscape.

Consciousness is "co-eternal," he said, with the natural world—"one self-same reality." This isn't a metaphor but rather a natural, neurological fact. Both a thought and a thing are products of energy, and so both are equally "real." Thus, to care for the outer landscape is to care for the inner. Both need to heal. Any show of empathy is a recognition that each landscape depends on the other. All of our environmental problems stem from a warped sense of self—a self at once diminished and unreasonably inflated. We refuse to understand self as something beyond the fortress of our own skin and ego, and yet we elevate our species with a domineering self-importance that is undeserved. One needs to expand while the other contracts. We always and never step in the same river twice. The face we had before we were born is the reflection we always see in the rivers. It is our primordial identification with the river itself—with nature's God.

The last two ideas I think we must hold together are what philosophers call the *vita activa* and the *vita contemplativa*—the active and the contemplative life. To my way of thinking, the contemplative life is one of private stillness and pregnant silence. Sometimes I sit on a rock outcrop above Clear Creek and affix my attention to a single trillium. Sometimes I sit on the floor of my small office and stare at the famous image of planet Earth taken from space—the swirling white clouds, the blue oceans, the green continents. A calm often overtakes me as I contemplate the microcosm of the trillium or the macrocosm of Earth. In that timeless moment of contemplation, I inhabit an intensely *aesthetic* mental landscape: I understand the beauty and the belongingness of this life experienced in direct relation to other subjects that are also—in both biological and intuitive ways—part of some larger self. The *vita contemplativa* is, as much as anything else, a mental state of attention and appreciation, it seems to me. That appreciation—"What to make of a diminished thing?"—leads me inevitably to the *vita activa*. That is to say, the *aesthetic* experience leads me into the *ethical* experience—the actions I take to defend and extend the life around me. The *vita contemplativa* alone risks quietism and solipsism. The *vita activa* alone risks resentment, anger, and even insanity. Each needs the other.

We Americans are fortunate to have inherited a lineage of "practical philosophers," stretching from Emerson and Thoreau down to John Dewey, William James, Jane Addams, Martha Nussbaum, Cornel West, and Richard Rorty. All of these thinkers abandoned the Platonic tradition that says the role of philosophy is to find some metaphysical foundation that will provide ultimate answers. Plato famously cast artists and poets out of his utopian republic because he felt their work was a distraction from our pursuit of the ultimate, highest good. John Dewey called this expulsion a "supreme instance of intellectual ingratitude." For Dewey, art is not, or shouldn't be, "the beauty parlor of civilization." Rather, the art impulse leads us to ritual, which leads us to meaning—a meaning *in this world*. Art and evolutionary science—far from exclusionary disciplines—actually perform the same function of showing humans that we are inextricably part of the natural world rather than would-be angels waiting for transport to a higher realm of meaning. Nothing demonstrates this better than the cave art our ancestors painted forty thousand years ago. Those artists desperately wanted to find some spiritual, psychological, and biological connection to the bison, the bulls, the aurochs they painted. The fact that those Paleolithic artists also painted figures that were half-human and half-animal shows they didn't want to simply dominate or kill those other mammals. On some level, they wanted to *be* them. Nature's God is a shape-shifting god. So we tried to emulate this evolutionary metamorphosis by becoming the lion-men and lion-women in the oldest cave art. We were embracing the *many* as a way back to the one. We were trying to affirm that the creation-many is inseparable from the creator-one. For the cave painters, there was no subject and object. The only subject was being.

In a similar sense, evolutionary science shows us that humans are not superior creatures put on earth to "have dominion" over its nonhuman inhabitants. We are simply part of life's great and ongoing invention. "The sense of relation between nature and man in some form has always been the actuating spirit of art," writes Dewey in *Art as Experience.* Fear is a natural response to mystery. But wonder is another response. Wonder gives rise to art. The scientific impulse to know and the aesthetic impulse to embody other creatures are both spectacular acts of the imagination. So is our ability to consciously contemplate our place in the world and to ethically imagine a better way of inhabiting that world. To be a philosopher, wrote Thoreau, is not to found a school or think abstract thoughts; rather, it is "to love wisdom as to live according to its dictates, a life of simplicity, independence, magnanimity, and trust." If we think of philosophy as a way of being in the world, as opposed to merely existing in it, then we all possess the aesthetic and ethical resources to become the philosophers of our own lives—the makers of meaning that might elevate this one life to a level of intensity and clarity embodied in the great works of art.

IN A LETTER-POEM to a friend, John Keats spoke of "the fine Web of his Soul" that a human being might weave, "filling the air with a beautiful circuiting," if we weren't crippled by distraction, dishonesty, and dissension. But if we could ever, as a people, overcome our animus,

> Minds would leave each other in contrary directions,
> traverse each other in numberless points, and at last greet each
> other at the journey's end. An old Man and a child would talk
> together and the old Man be led on his path and the child left
> thinking. Man should not dispute or assert but whisper results
> to his neighbour and thus by every germ of spirit sucking the
> sap from mould ethereal every human might become great,
> and Humanity instead of being a wide heath of Furze and
> Briars with here and there a remote Oak or Pine, would
> become a grand democracy of Forest Trees!

A grand democracy of forest trees! A watershed confederacy writing its own constitution on the winds and in the soil. A culture—whether a silviculture or human culture—of neighborliness, congeniality, greatness. I sit on the edge of these woods surrounding Clear Creek and contemplate all the things a forest has to teach us about democracy: the importance of diversity, integrity, stability, thrift, subsistence, interdependence, cooperation, health. The philosopher Alfred North Whitehead once marveled, "A forest is the triumph of the organization of mutually dependent species." He was right. I think of the few solitary bur oaks and blue ashes standing in isolation up in the pastures along Sellers Mill Road. They have been badly wind-whipped and lightning-struck. Most are now dropping dying limbs and will soon die altogether. They have been left removed from the forest democracy, and though they grow larger than their woodland kin, they are paying the price for that resource wealth, that magnitude. I also think about Aldo Leopold, who was shocked in 1935 when he visited German forests and found that most had been managed only as single-tree monocultures. Forest birdlife was almost nonexistent, Leopold observed. But when small planes flew over the German forests decades later, they found dramatic symbols of what Leopold had already observed during the rise of fascism in Germany. Planted throughout the artificially engineered pine forests were swastikas. The swastika pattern took the form of larch trees that turned orange and brown in autumn, so their swastika formation could be easily seen from above in contrast to the evergreen pines. During the thirties, while Leopold was inspecting German forests,

German citizens were taking to the woods to plant the *very symbol* of a monoculture: the swastika. But as Leopold observed, Nazi "purity" is as unnatural as a forest made up of one species. Leopold returned to Wisconsin to begin replanting a native woodlot in Sauk County, which he called Sand County because ruinous farming methods had reduced earlier forests to a desert. Leopold worked until his death—helping a neighbor fight a fire—to restore a native American woodland: a grand democracy of forest trees. That charge should be our own—to restore the health of the American landscape at the same time we work to replant the saplings of a real democracy.

PERHAPS THE BEST day of the year is the day when I can finally move my office outside. Today, I'm again sitting on the deck in a slowly deteriorating Adirondack chair with my notebook and binoculars. Down below, a slope of forsythia has broken into bloom. The hens peck through straw in the aviary. After last night's rain, all the springs on the western slope have once more come to life. This morning, I watched three mystically sleek river otters diving over each other up in Clear Creek's deeper pool. The fat pink buds at the tip of each buckeye branch are about to break open into a pantomime of tiny hands, first russet and then chlorophyll-green. The small white flowers of hepatica have emerged on their short, slender stems, and Virginia bluebells tentatively poke small purple tongues out of their sepals. The year's first mourning cloak butterfly is hovering around the stone Buddha that sits on our railing, next to the bird feeders that are spinning with goldfinches, nuthatches, and chickadees.

Down below, I can hear the beautiful, liquid slur of the wood thrushes' song. Resurrection, I begin to think, is a miracle as common around here as bloodroot and baptisia. Soon, no doubt, that pair of summer tanagers will return once more to build their nest at the edge of these woods.